Ikigai Unveiled

The Japanese Secret to a Purposeful Life

Michael Sato

Table of Contents

INTRODUCTION

Finding real satisfaction and purpose is refreshingly presented by the ancient Japanese idea of Ikigai in a society where the quest for pleasure through material prosperity and social standing is becoming more and more prevalent. Deeply exploring this fundamental idea, "Ikigai Unveiled: The Japanese Secret to a Purposeful Life" contends that each person has a special reason for being that resides at the nexus of what they love, what they are excellent at, what the world needs, and what they may be compensated for. Through an exploration of the subtleties of Ikigai, this book gives readers the knowledge as well as skills necessary to find and develop their own Ikigai.

"Ikigai Unveiled" takes readers on a path of self-discovery and personal development through a combination of philosophical knowledge, useful activities, and anecdotes from actual lives. It shows how living an Ikigai-based life may be more balanced, purposeful, and happy. The book looks into the cultural origins of Ikigai in Okinawa, a place renowned for having a high percentage of centenarians, and learns from their ways of living.

"Ikigai Unveiled" also tackles typical roadblocks to identifying one's Ikigai, including social pressures, failure-apprehension, and the difficulty of juggling several obligations. It offers doable plans for including Ikigai into everyday life, from forming positive habits and fostering relationships to locating or starting a job that reflects one's own interests and beliefs.

More than simply a book, "Ikigai Unveiled: The Japanese Secret to a Purposeful Life" is a whole manual for leading a happy, resilient, and deeply satisfying existence. Readers are enabled to change their life and start a path of long-lasting joy and purpose by discovering the ageless knowledge of Ikigai.

CHAPTER I

Discovering Ikigai

Introduction to the concept of Ikigai

An old Japanese philosophy known as "Ikigai" has drawn a lot of attention lately for its profound influence on living a happy and meaningful life. Japanese in origin, Ikigai is sometimes referred to as "a reason for being" or "a reason to wake up in the morning." Offering a comprehensive strategy for creating a balanced and purposeful life, it embodies the meeting point of passion, mission, vocation, and career.

Ikigai is essentially the combination of four basic components: what you enjoy, what you are excellent at, what the world needs, and what you can be compensated for. Ikigai is the essence of these factors coming together to indicate that matching one's talents and interests with a larger goal that also offers financial security is the path to real pleasure and contentment. Finding a good career and engaging in hobbies are only two components of this complex balance; the other is combining all facets of life to produce a peaceful and fulfilling life.

Ikigai originally appeared in literary works to characterize the pleasures and life satisfaction that come from ordinary encounters throughout Japan's Heian period (794–1185 AD). Ikigai developed across generations, being ingrained in Japanese everyday life and culture. It is a reflection of a worldview that stresses the need for both individual and group well-being and emphasizes the harmony between achieving personal fulfillment and serving society.

Knowing Ikigai means exploring each of its four parts. Your passions and interests are covered by the first element, what you adore. It's finding the passions, hobbies, and activities that make you happy and fulfilled. This aspect of Ikigai invites introspection to find out what really motivates and thrills you. It is about identifying those times when you are totally engrossed and happy with what you are doing.

What you are excellent at is the second element and it has to do with your abilities, talents, and strong points. It is about realizing and using your special skills to add value. This aspect of Ikigai demands an open evaluation of your talents and a desire to keep getting better. It is about discovering methods to succeed and becoming experts in specific subjects, not just about being good at them.

What the world needs is the third element, which talks about the larger picture of your life and your potential to benefit society. It is determining which possibilities, issues, and needs in the world speak to you and where you can have a significant influence. This aspect of Ikigai is about discovering a reason to live that transcends self-satisfaction and is in line with a larger good. It promotes service and responsibility and makes people think about how their deeds could help other people and make a good difference.

The practical part of maintaining your living is covered by the fourth component, what you can be compensated for. Finding methods to make money from your interests and talents is part of it. This aspect of Ikigai makes sure that long-term sustainability of following your interests and purpose is ensured by acknowledging the need of economic stability. It is about developing a profession or calling that satisfies your financial requirements in addition to your personal demands.

The beauty of Ikigai is in its integrative character, where the accomplishment of one element improves the others. Pursuing your passion, for example, could help you enhance your skills, which will enable you to make a more meaningful contribution to the world. Comparably, figuring out how to be compensated for the things you enjoy and excel at guarantees that your endeavor will last, and you can keep having a wonderful influence. This interdependence starts a positive circle that advances general happiness and well-being.

The idea of Ikigai provides a novel and all-encompassing method of achieving balance and meaning in contemporary society, where the pace of life is frequently busy, and the demands to achieve may be overpowering. It invites people to take a moment to consider their actual goals and strong points and to match their deeds with a bigger picture. In this way, Ikigai promotes inner tranquility and happiness, which lowers stress and improves the general quality of life.

Ikigai is not, after all, a universal concept. It is quite personal and particular to every person. What is Ikigai to one person could not be at all to another. Ikigai is a fluid and adaptable ideology that everyone, from any background or situation, may accept because of this personalization. It's about paving your own route and creating your own idea of a meaningful existence.

Beyond the domain of individual fulfillment, Ikigai finds use in organizational and professional settings. Ikigai concepts are currently being used by many companies and executives to build more meaningful work environments. Organizations may promote increased involvement, productivity, and work happiness by assisting staff members in finding and pursuing their Ikigai. This strategy helps people personally and also helps the company succeed and last long in general.

In actual life, finding your Ikigai is an ongoing process of introspection and experimenting. It calls for receptivity to novel experiences, a readiness to take chances, and the guts to adapt when called for. It's about being aware of your inner wants and talents and yet being aware of the opportunities and needs in your immediate environment. Both difficult and fulfilling, this path of learning can result in deep understanding and long-lasting change.

All things considered, Ikigai provides a potent foundation for living a meaningful and happy life. Ikigai offers a comprehensive method to finding balance and meaning by combining your passions, your skills, what the world needs, and what you can be compensated for. Given its roots in Japanese culture and its applicability to contemporary living, it is a timeless concept that anybody wishing to live a happy and fulfilling life may embrace. By means of ongoing introspection and matching of interests, talents, goals, and financial security, Ikigai promotes inner tranquility, resiliency, and general well-being, directing people toward a life of genuine pleasure and satisfaction.

Exploring the origins of Ikigai in Japanese culture

Ikigai initially appeared in Japanese literature during the Heian period (794–1185), when Japanese art, literature, and culture flourished. The nobility during this time, especially the court nobles, supported a rich cultural milieu via their creative and intellectual endeavors. As part of this cultural environment, the idea of Ikigai developed, expressing the focus on finding happiness and pleasure in the little things in life. Ikigai was first understood in part because of the literary works of the Heian period, which frequently portrayed the beauty of nature, the grace of court life, and the quest for aesthetic pleasure.

Murasaki Shikibu's "The Tale of Genji" is among the most important Heian era pieces illustrating the idea of Ikigai. Thought to be among the first books ever written, "The Tale of Genji" delves into themes of beauty, love, and the fleeting essence of life while examining the lives and loves of Prince Genji, the main character. The book emphasizes the quest for personal satisfaction and the enjoyment of the present moment, two essential elements of the idea of Ikigai, through its complex story and thorough depictions of courtly life.

Traditional Japanese religions and philosophies, including Shintoism and Buddhism, are also where Ikigai first appeared. The lessons of mindfulness, impermanence, and the quest for enlightenment were brought to Japan with Buddhism when it was first taught there in the sixth century. Ikigai and Japanese culture were greatly impacted by these beliefs. Ikigai is based on the Buddhist notion of "shojin," or the quest for perfection and self-improvement, in which people work to discover and develop their life's purpose via ongoing development and introspection.

Ikigai is also greatly influenced by Shintoism, the native religion of Japan. Nature, spirituality, and the interdependence of all living things are all highly valued in Shintoism. The Shinto faith in the "kami," or spirits, present in trees, mountains, and rivers, promotes a profound respect for the natural environment and exhorts people to live in peace and balance. Understanding Ikigai requires respect for nature and an emphasis on coexisting peacefully with one's environment.

The social and cultural principles underlying Ikigai were further cemented throughout the Edo era (1603–1868). Japan's economy grew, and its arts and culture flourished during this time of comparatively calm and stability under the Tokugawa shogunate. During the Edo era, the merchant class rose to prominence and ukiyo-e (woodblock prints), kabuki theater, and haiku poetry all flourished. The focus placed at this time on craftsmanship, aesthetic enjoyment, and following one's own interests helped to expand the concept of Ikigai.

The Edo-era idea of "mono no aware" is intimately connected to Ikigai. Translating to "pathos of things," "mono no aware" describes the knowledge of life's fleeting nature and the beauty inherent in that impermanence. This attitude exhorts people to enjoy the little moments in life and to treasure the present. Appreciating "mono no aware" is consistent with Ikigai's tenets, which emphasize enjoyment and significance in the small, sometimes disregarded parts of everyday life.

Ikigai has also been greatly impacted by the Japanese work ethic and the idea of "shokunin," which describes a craftsman or artisan who is committed to their trade and aspires to master it. The concept of "shokunin" captures the essence of Ikigai, in which people, through their labor and the quest for excellence, find meaning and fulfillment. The "shokunin" mindset and the principles that support Ikigai are typified by a devotion to one's trade, attention to detail, and ongoing progress.

Ikigai is still a prominent idea in everyday living and cultural identity in contemporary Japan. It is evident in a number of facets of Japanese culture, from the painstaking attention to detail in traditional tea rituals to the commitment and pride shown in routine chores, whether at home or at work. The Japanese concept of work-life balance, "karoshi" (death by overwork), has also brought attention to the necessity of a more comprehensive conception of happiness and well-being, hence highlighting the significance of Ikigai in modern living.

Beyond personal goals, Ikigai influences Japanese society norms and communal life. Central to Japanese culture, the idea of "wa," or harmony, stresses the need of preserving harmony and balance inside the society. Ikigai supports people in discovering their own purpose and using it to further the common good. One distinguishing quality of Ikigai, which reflects the collective spirit of Japanese society, is the interdependence of individual fulfillment and social harmony.

Ikigai has become well-known worldwide in recent years and appeals to individuals from all cultural origins. This broad interest is explained by the rising knowledge of the value of mental health and well-being, as well as the need of finding purpose in a world that is becoming more and more linked and fast-paced. Across many cultures and situations, the ideas of Ikigai provide a timeless and universal foundation for reaching balance and contentment.

Ikigai has been studied in many publications and research, which has clarified its meaning and usefulness. Among the most well-known is Francesc Miralles and Héctor García's "Ikigai: The Japanese Secret to a Long and Happy Life." The writers explore the secrets of the longevity and happiness of the people living on Okinawa, a Japanese island well-known for having a high percentage of centenarians. By means of their studies, they demonstrate how the Okinawan people's lifespan and well-being are enhanced by the Ikigai tenets, which include a strong feeling of community, a healthy lifestyle, and a distinct purpose.

Beyond the realm of individual well-being, Ikigai finds use in organizational and professional settings. The ideas of Ikigai have been accepted by many companies and leaders in order to improve employee happiness and engagement and to create more meaningful work environments. Organizations may develop a culture of purpose, creativity, and resilience by enabling staff members to find and follow their Ikigai. This strategy helps people personally as well as the general performance and long-term viability of the company.

In education, Ikigai concepts may motivate and direct pupils in their academic and personal endeavors. Young people may lay a solid basis for a happy and purposeful life through instructors who inspire them to follow their passions, hone their talents, and look for opportunities to benefit society. Ikigai may be included in the curriculum to promote creativity, curiosity, and social responsibility in pupils, therefore equipping them to deal with the complexity of the contemporary world.

When one examines Ikigai in Japanese culture, one finds a complex and multidimensional philosophy that includes peace in society, personal fulfillment, and a profound respect for the present. Ikigai has developed and is understood in part because of its Heian period roots, Buddhist and Shintoistic influences, and Edo period cultural norms. Being an ageless and universal idea, Ikigai is relevant and approachable to people everywhere since it provides insightful advice and useful advice for living a fulfilling and balanced life.

In summary, Ikigai has its roots firmly in the history, philosophy, and social ideals of Japan. From its earliest literary works of the Heian period to its Buddhist and Shintoistic inspirations and its embodiment in the work ethic and aesthetic appreciation of the Edo period, Ikigai represents a comprehensive and integrated approach to achieving happiness and purpose. The ideas of Ikigai offer a timeless and universal framework for finding balance, well-being, and happiness even while the world struggles with the problems of modern life. A more peaceful and fulfilling life can result from people developing a deeper awareness of themselves and their role in the world by investigating and accepting the idea of Ikigai.

Defining Ikigai: the intersection of passion, mission, vocation, and profession

First aspect of Ikigai, passion describes the joyous and fulfilling hobbies, interests, and endeavors. Passion is about your favorite things to do, the ones that engross you and cause you to lose all sense of time. Finding one's passions sometimes takes introspection and investigation of several topics. It's learning what motivates and thrills you, what gives you life and happiness. Passion exists in employment, relationships, and personal development in addition to hobbies and leisure pursuits. It's about recognizing and utilizing your own intrinsic desire for doing particular things, independent of outside incentives or acknowledgement.

Since it gives the emotional vigor and excitement required to start a path of self-discovery and satisfaction, passion is sometimes seen as the beginning point of Ikigai. People that are enthusiastic about what they do go into a state of flow, when they are totally absorbed and forget about time. Productivity, creativity, and enjoyment all rise with this state of flow. A foundation for a happy and meaningful life may be laid by people discovering and pursuing their hobbies.

The second component of Ikigai, mission, is the larger reason or goal that gives your life significance. It's seeing how your interests and skills may be applied to meet global needs and advance society. The essence of mission is discovering a reason to live that transcends personal fulfillment and is in line with a greater good or objective. It has to do with realizing your place in society and how your deeds and efforts might improve things.

One must consider their own goals, values, and beliefs in order to determine their purpose. It entails posing questions like, "What world problems or issues speak to me?" What causes or movements personally excite me? In what ways may I apply my abilities to change things? A feeling of social duty and service is intimately related to mission, which makes people think about how their deeds might help others and improve the world.

The third component of Ikigai, vocation, describes the job or career that fits your goals and desires. It's figuring out a job or line of work that lets you make significant and satisfying use of your abilities. Finding job that gives one a feeling of meaning and fulfillment in addition to financial security is called vocation. It is about bringing your mission and interests into your work life so that what you enjoy, what you are excellent at, and what the world needs are seamlessly connected.

Finding one's calling frequently calls for in-depth knowledge of one's own interests, talents, and abilities.

It's looking at several career paths and figuring out how to make your job fit your goals and hobbies. Finding a profession that fits your beliefs and enables you to make a positive contribution to society is more important to vocation than simply finding one that pays well. You may lead a happy and meaningful work life if your occupation fits with your Ikigai.

The fourth component of Ikigai, profession, is the way you really make a living. Finding methods to make money off of your interests and talents is part of it. Making a job or career that satisfies your financial demands in addition to your personal needs is the essence of profession. It is about striking a compromise between financial security and personal satisfaction so that your quest of Ikigai is long-term viable.

One should take into account the market need for their abilities and skills as well as the financial feasibility of their selected career route while determining their occupation. It's knowing the state of the economy and figuring out how to use your goals and hobbies to build a steady stream of income. Finding a realistic and workable path to follow your Ikigai and making sure you can provide for your family and yourself while working in a job you enjoy is what makes a career.

Ikigai is the meeting point of career, vocation, purpose, and passion. People discover their actual meaning and fulfillment where these four components come together. This junction is dynamic and changing; it needs ongoing introspection, investigation, and modification. Discovering your interests, comprehending your purpose, recognizing your calling, and building a sustainable career are all part of the self-discovery process that is finding your Ikigai.

Deeply embedded in Japanese culture, the idea of Ikigai represents the principles of balance, harmony, and interconnection. It highlights the need of bringing happiness and meaning into daily activities and the conviction that real fulfillment results from combining one's talents and interests with a larger societal goal. Ikigai is about improving the world and improving the lives of others, not only about oneself.

In actual life, discovering your Ikigai is an ongoing process of introspection and experimenting. It calls for receptivity to novel experiences, a readiness to take chances, and the guts to adapt when called for. It's about being aware of your inner wants and talents and yet being aware of the opportunities and needs in your immediate environment. Deep discoveries and long-lasting transformation can result from this demanding yet fulfilling path of inquiry.

Starting with introspection is one doable way to locate your Ikigai. Investigate your hobbies and passions and note the things that make you happy and fulfilled. Think on your innate abilities and the abilities and skills you have acquired throughout time. Consider the causes or problems that speak to you, then think about how you may utilize your skills to change the world. Ultimately, look at several job paths and think about how to sustainably make money from your interests and abilities.

Getting opinions and direction from others is another strategy. Talk to people about your talents and possible professional routes—friends, family, mentors, and coworkers. Look for chances to develop personally and be willing to try new things. Developing a variety of viewpoints and experiences can help you to see fresh opportunities and improve your comprehension of your Ikigai.

Choosing deliberately and forming habits that support your interests, mission, vocation, and career are how you incorporate Ikigai into your everyday life. It's establishing priorities and objectives that align with your beliefs and dreams and acting in ways that advance you toward your

Ikigai. This can be changing your work, taking up a new pastime, or volunteering in the community. Taking up self-care, mindfulness, and gratitude as well as other techniques to promote your general happiness and well-being may also be included.

Locating and living your Ikigai has several advantages. More than financial success, you have a feeling of purpose and fulfillment when your interests, mission, vocation, and career are in line. You are more resilient in the face of obstacles and disappointments and feel more involved and driven in your everyday pursuits. Since your deeds improve the welfare of your neighborhood and the planet, you also feel more harmony and connection with other people.

Living your Ikigai can also help you be healthier both physically and mentally. A feeling of purpose has been linked in research to increased levels of pleasure and life satisfaction as well as decreased levels of stress and sadness. Better physical health—including a reduced chance of chronic illnesses and a higher life expectancy—is also associated with it. Your whole health and quality of life can be improved by discovering and pursuing your Ikigai.

Apart from the advantages to oneself, the Ikigai concepts may be used in organizational and professional settings to provide more meaningful work environments. Ikigai concepts have been accepted by many companies and executives to improve productivity, contentment, and employee engagement. Organizations may develop a culture of purpose, creativity, and resilience by enabling staff members to find and follow their Ikigai. This strategy helps the company succeed generally and sustainably in addition to benefiting the person.

Businesses might, for instance, provide chances for staff members to investigate their interests and strong points through flexible work schedules, mentoring, and professional development programs. Employees can also feel a feeling of duty and shared purpose when their mission and values are in line with more general social and environmental objectives. Higher engagement and performance can result from companies helping their staff members find purpose and fulfillment in their job by creating a welcoming and encouraging work environment.

Ikigai's tenets can motivate and direct pupils in their academic and personal endeavors. Young people may lay a solid basis for a happy and purposeful life by instructors who inspire them to follow their passions, hone their talents, and look for opportunities to benefit society. Ikigai may be included into curriculum to promote creativity, curiosity, and social responsibility in pupils, therefore equipping them to deal with the complexity of the contemporary world.

Ikigai, then, offers a comprehensive framework for achieving purpose and fulfillment in life by representing the meeting point of passion, mission, vocation, and profession. Through knowledge of and integration of these four components, people may design a meaningful and balanced life that makes them happy and satisfied and benefits society at large. Though it takes ongoing introspection, investigation, and modification to discover and live your Ikigai, the benefits are great and far-reaching. Ikigai's tenets can help people live happier, healthier lives both physically and mentally, and in more meaningful work and organizational settings. You may design a life of real meaning and fulfillment that plays to your special talents and interests and advances society.

The importance of finding your Ikigai in modern life

The huge influence identifying your Ikigai has on your own well-being is the first reason it is so important in modern life. Finding one's Ikigai may be a potent cure in a society where mental health problems, including stress, worry, and depression, are becoming more and more common. People are happier and more satisfied when they participate in activities that play to their interests and strong points. Time appears to stop still, and they are totally absorbed in their activities, which is the source of this innate delight that results from doing what they love and being excellent at it. This is a very pleasant condition that also has great advantages for mental health, as it lowers stress and improves general well-being.

Emotional resilience is also much increased by having a strong sense of purpose, which is essential to the idea of Ikigai. People are better able to handle obstacles and disappointments in life when they are aware of their wider purpose in life and how their deeds support a bigger cause. This feeling of purpose helps to prevent hardship and promotes a more upbeat and proactive attitude to problem-solving. It gives people purpose and direction that ground them in the middle of the uncertainty of contemporary life, resulting in increased emotional stability and a more optimistic view.

Finding your Ikigai not only improves your own well-being but also is essential to success and professional fulfillment. High demands, fast changes, and fierce rivalry are common characteristics of the modern workplace. In such a situation, the conventional method of looking for steady and safe work only for financial reasons is becoming less and less effective. Rather, a more satisfying and long-lasting professional existence results from coordinating one's work with one's interests, abilities, and values—the core of Ikigai. People who follow professions they are enthusiastic about and that make use of their special skills are more likely to be satisfied at work and to remain motivated over time.

Ikigai can also help one be more creative and innovative in their work life. Real love for what they do makes people more inclined to think imaginatively, take initiative, and push the envelope of what is thought feasible. Higher levels of performance and accomplishment result from ongoing learning and development driven by this inner desire. Organizations that support their staff members in discovering and pursuing their Ikigai frequently gain from a more motivated and productive workforce that promotes innovation and excellence.

Ikigai emphasizes especially the value of society's contribution and the interdependence between personal welfare and the welfare of the community. In today's world of social disintegration and isolation, finding methods to further the greater good can help one feel purposeful and like they belong. Ikigai promotes social responsibility and group well-being by asking people to think about how their interests and talents could serve the needs of the world. This emphasis on social responsibility unites personal satisfaction with the more general objective of bettering the world, hence establishing a positive cycle in which the welfare of the individual and society is mutually reinforcing.

Further, the quest of Ikigai can result in the creation of more sympathetic and compassionate civilizations. People who are involved in fulfilling jobs that uphold their principles and advance society are more prone to grow in empathy and compassion for others. Beyond intimate connections, this empathy includes a wider concern for social and environmental concerns. Greater social cohesiveness, lower inequality, and a more sustainable and just world can all result from the collective influence on society as more individuals discover and embody their Ikigai.

Finding your Ikigai is crucial in today's world of personal growth and education as well. In a time when conventional educational methods are being called into question, Ikigai's ideas provide a more comprehensive and customized approach to development. Teachers may provide a solid basis for a happy and purposeful life by urging pupils to follow their passions, hone their special skills, and comprehend their place in society. With this method, students develop a passion for learning, internal drive, and a feeling of accountability, which equips them to confidently and resiliently negotiate the complexity of contemporary society.

Including Ikigai in the classroom also tackles the mounting worry about the disconnect between academic programs and practical demands. Teachers may design more relevant and interesting learning experiences by matching the abilities society demands and the interests of their students with the curriculum. Together with improving student success and engagement, this alignment guarantees that students are better equipped for the possibilities and challenges of the future. The ideas of Ikigai can, therefore, turn education into a more significant and worthwhile undertaking that will help people and society at large.

Building communities and personal connections arc also greatly impacted by the quest of Ikigai. Identifying one's Ikigai helps strengthen social bonds and foster a feeling of community in contemporary cultures where social isolation and loneliness are prevalent problems. People are more prone to build deeper and more genuine connections when they are involved in worthwhile activities that complement their passions and ideals. People coming together for the same objectives and causes strengthen this sense of connection even more, encouraging support and solidarity.

Furthermore, by encouraging empathy, compassion, and understanding between people, the ideas of Ikigai can improve the caliber of interpersonal interactions. People who are in line with their Ikigai are more inclined to approach relationships with purpose and deliberateness.

Deeper knowledge of oneself and others that results from this alignment makes interactions more meaningful and satisfying. Ikigai may make personal interactions joyful, supportive, and growth-promoting by putting connection and contribution first, therefore improving people's lives and the social fabric.

Locating one's Ikigai can have a big impact on one's physical and emotional well-being. A feeling of purpose has been linked in research to a number of health advantages, including improved cardiovascular health, longer life expectancy, and reduced stress and depression. People can feel better generally and have more energy when their lives are in line with their interests, talents, and values. This all-encompassing approach to health stresses the need to live in accordance with one's own self and acknowledges the interdependence of the mind, body, and spirit.

Ikigai's tenets also encourage good behaviors and life decisions. People are more inclined to take up habits that promote their well-being, like frequent exercise, nutritious diet, and stress management techniques when they are involved in worthwhile activities and feel clearly purposeful. Living in accordance with one's Ikigai gives one a sense of pleasure and happiness that strengthens these good habits even more. Ikigai can increase lifespan and improve quality of life by encouraging a comprehensive approach to health and wellness.

Broadly speaking, Ikigai's ideals can help create more egalitarian and sustainable communities. Ikigai encourages people to match their own happiness with their contribution to society, therefore fostering a feeling of duty and stewardship. More sustainable methods in social justice, economic growth, and environmental protection can result from this strategy. People may effect good change and build a more sustainable and equitable world if they can use their special skills and interests to further the greater good.

The Ikigai principles may also guide governance and policy-making, encouraging more comprehensive and inclusive approaches to society's well-being. Understanding the value of both individual fulfillment and social service, legislators may design systems that help people discover and live their Ikigai. In the end, people and society as a whole can gain from more thorough and efficient policies in fields like social services, healthcare, and education.

Finding your Ikigai is a very personal and always changing process. It calls on ongoing introspection, investigation, and adjustment. This path is more vital than ever in the contemporary world of unpredictability and ongoing change. Adopting the Ikigai concepts helps people to more clearly, purposefully, and resiliently negotiate the complexity of modern life.

Finding your Ikigai practically may be done via self-discovery and exploration. This is looking at several pastimes, interests, and professional options to see what really speaks to you. It takes guts and a readiness to venture outside of your comfort zone and follow your hobbies and aspirations. This investigative trip may be gratifying and demanding at the same time, producing deep understanding and long-lasting change.

Finding your Ikigai also involves getting advice and criticism from others. Talking with friends, family, mentors, and coworkers may provide you with important new views on your interests, talents, and possible professional pathways. Your comprehension of your Ikigai may be improved, and you can get closer to a life of meaning and fulfillment by looking for chances for learning and development and being receptive to new experiences.

Pursuing Ikigai also entails choosing deliberately and developing routines that support your interests, purpose, vocation, and career. This might include deciding on priorities and objectives that align with your beliefs and dreams and acting in ways that advance you toward your Ikigai. It can also mean changing your work, taking up a new pastime, or volunteering in the community. Living in harmony with your Ikigai and developing behaviors that promote your contentment and well-being can help you to have a more meaningful and balanced life.

In summary, identifying your Ikigai provides a foundation for achieving personal happiness, job fulfillment, and social contribution and is thus very important in contemporary life. A life of meaning and fulfillment may be created by lining up your passions, talents, needs, and ability to be compensated for. Ikigai's tenets foster social responsibility, creativity, emotional resilience, and better mental and physical health as well as more robust interpersonal connections and more just and sustainable societies. It takes constant introspection, research, and deliberate decision-making to discover and live your Ikigai. Through accepting this path, you may more clearly, purposefully, and resiliently negotiate the complexity of contemporary life, therefore building a life that is really worthwhile.

CHAPTER II

The Four Pillars of Ikigai

What You Love: Exploring passions and interests
The foundation of a happy life is interests and passions. They give us delight and a feeling of purpose. They mold our identities and motivate our behavior. Discovering what you love is a voyage of self-discovery that may result in significant personal and professional development, not only a pursuit of hobbies. This paper explores the value of passions and interests, how to recognize them, how they affect our lives, and how to develop and include them in our everyday activities.

Strong motivators and passions steer us toward certain hobbies, causes, or goals. They are the things we find fundamentally satisfying that excite us and that cause us to lose track of time. Conversely, interests are more broad propensities toward certain topics or activities. While interests might vary considerably and alter over time, passions are frequently strong and lasting. In forming our life and enhancing our general well-being, both are essential.

One cannot stress the need to pursue hobbies and passions enough. Taking part in things we enjoy does make us happy and satisfied, which is a much-needed diversion from the pressures and stresses of everyday living. It increases our sense of accomplishment and our self-esteem. Furthermore, following our hobbies could help us to acquire new abilities and skills, which might lead to chances we would not have otherwise had.

The first on this path is figuring out what you enjoy. Reflection and a readiness to take chances are part of this process. One might get important hints by thinking back on happy and satisfying former events and activities. Subtle passions and interests can be found by asking questions like "What activities make me lose track of time?" or "What topics do I find myself constantly curious about?" Get input from friends and family as well; they frequently notice our tendencies and actions more dispassionately and might provide insights we might miss.

Finding our interests also involves trying new things and venturing beyond of our comfort zones. Taking up a new activity, picking up a musical instrument, volunteering for a cause, or going to seminars and workshops—trying new activities might uncover interests you never knew you had. Because it lets us try a variety of things and find out what really speaks to us, this exploration stage is essential .

Having found our hobbies and interests, it is important to incorporate them into our daily lives. Particularly when job, family, and other obligations are on your plate, this can be difficult. To be healthy overall, though, we must put our loves first. Even little changes in including these activities in our everyday schedules can add up to a big difference. Effective tactics are to discover methods to integrate our hobbies into our work life, join clubs or groups with like interests, and set aside a specific time each week for our passions.

The influence of following hobbies and passions goes beyond the gratification of the individual. It lessens stress and worry and improves our mental and emotional health. By stimulating the brain, doing things we enjoy encourages creativity and problem-solving abilities. Because we frequently encounter people who have similar interests, it also promotes a feeling of belonging and community. Through their encouragement, support, and sense of community, these social ties may significantly improve our lives.

Interests and passions may also have a big impact on our professional choices. Many accomplished people have made gratifying careers out of their interests. Passionate about what we do, we are more likely to be driven, productive, and resilient under pressure. Because we are ready to devote the time and energy required to reach our objectives, work motivated by passion frequently results in innovation and greatness. As such, coordinating our professional paths with our interests can increase both job happiness and general success.

It is critical to understand, nonetheless, that following hobbies and passions is not always easy. Along the road, there might be roadblocks and disappointments. Common obstacles that prevent us from completely pursuing our hobbies are fear of failing, time limits, financial limitations, and social expectations. It takes tenacity, imagination, and perhaps a readiness to make concessions to overcome these obstacles.

For many, one major barrier is their fear of failing. It might be intimidating to think that you could fail or that people would think poorly of you. Failure must, therefore, be seen as a teaching moment rather than a setback. Overcoming this dread can be accomplished by adopting a growth mentality, in which we view obstacles as chances for personal progress. It may also be quite beneficial to surround oneself with encouraging people who push us to follow our passions.

Another important component is time management. Trying to fit in our hobbies might seem hard given the many demands on our time. Being aware of our time and giving what is really important priority is essential. This can be defining limits, assigning work, or even giving up on things that don't advance our general well-being. Our hobbies may also be accommodated with the use of time management strategies and tools like making timetables and establishing clear objectives.

One other obstacle might be money, particularly if our desires call for a large outlay of funds. But there are usually innovative approaches to follow hobbies without going over budget. Resources and programs are available for little or no cost from many community centers, libraries, and internet sites. Moreover, looking for sponsorships, grants, or scholarships might offer financial assistance for following particular hobbies. Popular methods for people to finance their artistic projects include also crowdsourcing and patronage models.

Our decisions and deterrents from following our true passions might come from society expectations and pressures. Maintaining our integrity and stifling the will to live up to expectations from others is crucial. This calls on self-awareness and self-assurance in our own goals and principles. Locating communities with similar minds and role models who have effectively followed their hobbies may be motivating and encouraging.

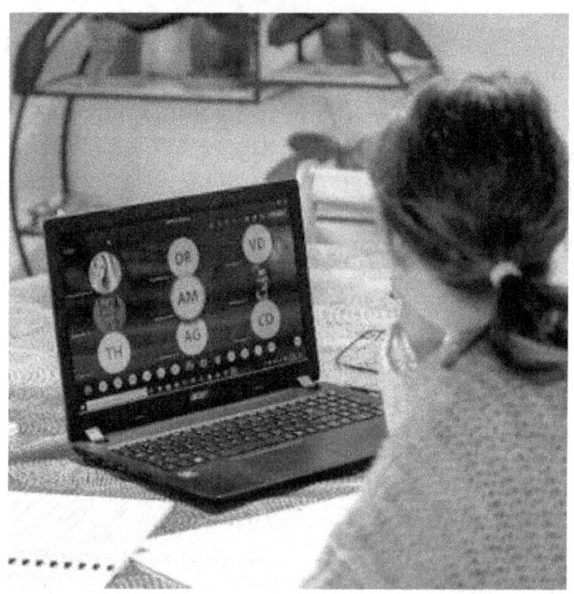

Another difficulty many have is juggling obligations and hobbies. It is crucial to fulfill our responsibilities and keep our lives stable, even if it is equally necessary to follow our goals. The key is to strike a balance between the two. This might be including our hobbies in our everyday activities in a way that enhances our obligations. For instance, setting out a few hours each week to write might be a sensible strategy if you love to write but work a full-time job.

It is never too late to start investigating hobbies and passions. New passions may surface, and our interests may shift as we mature. It's essential that we let ourselves develop and be receptive to these changes. Passions and interests are probably reflections of the dynamic process that is life. Continual personal development and enrichment can result from being open to new experiences and interests.

Besides, following hobbies and emotions has advantages for those outside of oneself. Communities and organizations that foster and aid in the interests of their members can benefit greatly. Promoting a culture at work that respects the hobbies and passions of staff members can boost motivation, creativity, and job happiness. All things considered, this can improve success and productivity generally. Comparably, communities that let people follow their passions may provide a lively and dynamic atmosphere that is advantageous to everybody.

Interests and passions are also often nurtured in large part by educational institutions. Encouragement of pupils to investigate a variety of topics and pursuits might assist them in early life in identifying their interests. Offering tools, guidance, and chances for practical experiences may promote a passion for learning and a feeling of purpose. Students who are enthusiastic about their studies are more likely to succeed academically and create a lifetime love of learning.

Finally, a key component of leading a happy and meaningful life is pursuing hobbies and interests. It is an exploration, experimenting, and tenacious trip within oneself. Finding our passion, incorporating it into our lives, and getting beyond challenges may result in significant personal and professional development. Beyond only enhancing our own happiness, following our passions improves our general quality of life, professional success, and mental and emotional health. Setting our loves first and being receptive to new experiences can help us live happier, more active lives.

What You Are Good At: Identifying skills and talents

A critical component of both professional and also personal growth is skill and talent identification. It entails realizing and appreciating your special talents, your areas of strength, and the special contributions you may give to society. Knowing your skills helps you to match your life with them and succeed more in life, not only progress your work. A life with more meaning and purpose can result from this transforming self-discovery experience. Knowing your abilities and talents is more crucial than ever in a world evolving quickly and where flexibility and lifelong learning are essential.

Though they are sometimes used synonymously, skills and talents have different meanings. Usually, one acquires skills from education, training, and experience. They are the abilities that, like programming, project management, or speaking a foreign language well, maybe honed over time. Conversely, talents are inherent skills or aptitudes that some people possess more readily than others. Examples are a love of music, an inbuilt grasp of difficult mathematical ideas, or outstanding people skills. You are good at what you do because of both abilities and talents, which frequently cross and enhance one another.

Reflection is the first step in discovering your abilities. This reflective approach entails a review of your prior accomplishments, experiences, and comments from others. Thinking back on your achievements can point up trends and provide an understanding of the things you do best naturally. Think back to the jobs or initiatives that have most satisfied and recognized you. You enjoyed what you did. Where did people compliment or acknowledge you? Important hints regarding your areas of strength and competence can be found in this contemplation.

Getting input from others is a further useful way to recognize abilities and capabilities. You may not have thought about some of the viewpoints that friends, family, coworkers, and mentors may provide. They can point up advantages you might not have seen and offer helpful criticism on areas that need work. Talking to others honestly and openly about your skills will help you realize your strengths more fully. Professional evaluations and personality tests, including StrengthsFinder or the Myers-Briggs Type Indicator (MBTI), can also offer organized information on your interests and skills. These instruments will enable you to recognize your strongest suit and how to use them in various situations.

Finding your strengths and skills also requires taking "flow" into account. Flow, so named by psychologist Mihaly Csikszentmihalyi, is the condition of being totally absorbed and involved in an activity to the point where time seems to stand still and engagement seems natural. Flow-promoting activities frequently complement your inherent abilities. Thinking back on times you've flowed might reveal a lot about your strengths and hobbies. These encounters may help you recognize your talents and are signs of activities that fit your interests and skill set.

Skills are developed and refined in large part by education and lifelong learning. Although formal education gives one basic knowledge and abilities in many areas, learning never ends. By means of classes, seminars, certificates, and independent study, lifelong learning enables you to always broaden and improve your skill set. Developing new skills and identifying hidden abilities might result from remaining inquisitive and receptive to new experiences. This proactive attitude to learning guarantees that, in a world changing quickly, your skills stay applicable and flexible.

Additionally, useful tools for recognizing and enhancing abilities and skills are coaching and mentoring. From their own experiences and areas of competence, mentors, and coaches may offer direction, encouragement, and criticism. They can assist you with goal-setting, problem-solving, and skill development action plans. Working with a coach or mentor may quicken your development and make it clear what your areas of strength and weakness are. In addition, this partnership might provide chances for networking and professional development, thereby extending your abilities.

Finding and honing talents may be done rather well at work. Opportunities to put your skills to use and evaluate them in practical situations are presented by professional experiences, projects, and partners. Your preferences and strong points may be seen by seeing how you perform in various jobs and responsibilities. Seek a variety of experiences and accept tasks that force you to step outside of your comfort zone. You get an understanding of the spectrum of your talents and places where you shine from this exposure. Performance reviews and comments from the workplace may provide offer organized insights into your areas of strength and improvement.

More ways to find and develop skills and abilities are via volunteering and community service. Volunteering enables you to use your skills in several settings and have a good influence. It offers chances to investigate new hobbies, hone new abilities, and obtain expertise in fields that you would not have access to in your work life. Participating in the community also helps one feel connected and purposeful, which improves general happiness and well-being. Giving to organizations you support can help you hone your current abilities and find new ones.

Often, signs of special abilities include creativity and inventiveness. Creative pursuits include writing, painting, music, and problem-solving call for the creative and innovative use of abilities. Creative activities may give chances for self-expression and personal development as well as expose hidden skills. It promotes unconventional thinking and viewpoints, which could reveal fresh talents. Your capacity to recognize and use your abilities may be improved by cultivating a creative attitude and looking for chances for invention.

It's equally crucial to understand that abilities and skills can change with time. New skills can be developed or current ones refined via life events, personal development, and interest changes. For continuous personal and professional growth, one must be adaptable and open to adjust. Reevaluating your abilities and skills on a regular basis helps you to stay in line with your strengths and be able to adjust to new chances and difficulties. This dynamic method of self-awareness and growth keeps you interested and driven all of your life.

For a thorough picture of your strengths, you must know the distinction between hard and soft talents. Hard skills, including language, technical, and academic knowledge, are particular, teachable talents that can be assessed and quantified. Conversely, soft skills are behavioral and interpersonal characteristics that shape your attitude to work and interactions with people. Soft talents include, for instance, emotional intelligence, leadership, teamwork, and communication. Both hard and soft talents are valuable, and learning to balance them may improve your performance and effectiveness in a variety of settings.

Finding and using your talents and abilities need self-awareness. It is knowing your values, motives, strengths, and shortcomings. Knowing yourself well helps you to choose wisely in both your personal and professional lives, matching your deeds to your talents and objectives. It also helps you to look for chances that play to your advantage and stay clear of circumstances where your shortcomings might work against you. It takes regular introspection, criticism, and a readiness to face and grow from your experiences to become self-aware.

It is impossible to overestimate the importance of enthusiasm in discovering abilities and capabilities. Motivated, persistent, and enthusiastic, passion propels you to succeed in pursuits that are in line with your interests. When something is important to you, you will probably put in more time and effort to learn relevant skills and overcome obstacles. Deeper involvement and greater accomplishments frequently result from passionate activities. Knowing your passion may help you find your special gifts and abilities, which will bring your life into harmony and meaning.

Finding and enhancing your abilities and talents may also be accomplished via networking and forming connections with others in your area of interest. Getting to know experts, becoming a member of trade associations, and going to conferences can provide you with an understanding of the abilities and qualities that are sought in your field of study. Getting fresh viewpoints, learning from others, and finding chances for personal improvement are all made possible via networking. Developing a solid professional network may also lead to fresh opportunities and teamwork that will improve your abilities.

Failures and obstacles provide priceless teaching moments as one searches for and hone their abilities and talents. Overcoming challenges can highlight talents you may not have realized and offer chances for development. Taking a resilient and optimistic attitude to obstacles might help you become more flexible and acquire new abilities. The approach must include learning from mistakes and disappointments as they reveal areas that need work and emphasize the need for tenacity and lifelong learning.

Setting objectives is a very effective method of honing abilities. Having defined, attainable objectives gives you direction and drive to concentrate your efforts on particular growth areas. Short-term goals include finishing a course or picking up a new skill; long-term goals include earning a professional certification or becoming an expert in a certain area. Goals provide an organized route for the development of your skills and your own development. Maintaining alignment with your abilities and making progress is ensured by routinely evaluating and modifying your goals.

Finally, knowing your strengths and abilities is the first step toward both career and personal fulfillment. It entails thinking back on oneself, getting input, pursuing hobbies, and actively participating in a range of situations. Knowing your abilities and talents goes beyond simply advancing in your work to include coordinating your life with your passions and strengths, which will increase your happiness and success.

Talents are inborn skills that people possess naturally; skills are learned via education, training, and experience. Both are quite important in forming your skills and your contribution to the world. It is critical to understand the distinction between hard and soft talents as both are required to successfully negotiate various professional and personal situations.

What the World Needs: Finding purpose and mission

In a world of fast technical progress, worldwide connectivity, and hitherto unseen difficulties, the search for meaning and purpose is more important than ever. Finding meaning becomes essential to human existence as civilizations change and people struggle with the intricacies of contemporary living. This section explores the complexity of purpose and goal, analyzing their importance for society and individuals alike and how they could effect constructive change in a world growing more unpredictable by the day.

Philosophers have studied purpose for a very long time. Aristotle, for example, proposed that a life well-lived is one that is directed by a sense of purpose, or telos. These days, as individuals try to make sense of the complexity of a world that is changing quickly, this idea has become even more important. Fundamentally, purpose gives people direction and a cause to exist that goes beyond the routine parts of everyday existence. It is the internal compass that directs choices, deeds, and goals, therefore promoting resilience and contentment.

Finding meaning mostly entails realizing one's own talents, interests, and moral principles. This path requires introspection and self-reflection as they help people find out what really important to them. In this process, one frequently has to dare to follow a path that is in line with their true selves and to challenge society standards and expectations. By this alignment, people may reach their greatest potential and improve both their personal and the community's well-being.

Purpose affects society's well-being profoundly, in addition to personal satisfaction. People driven by a feeling of purpose make for a society that is probably more cohesive, robust, and creative. Whether it be social fairness, environmental sustainability, or technical progress, individuals are more likely to cooperate and strive for shared objectives when they have a similar purpose. Divides may be healed, diversity promoted, and an atmosphere of understanding and support for one another created by this feeling of one purpose.

Purpose-driven people also frequently become change agents, questioning the existing quo and pushing for revolutionary answers to urgent global problems. Think about the influence of people like Malala Yousafzai, Martin Luther King Jr., and Mahatma Gandhi, whose unflinching dedication to their goals has motivated innumerable others and brought about tremendous social advancement. Their lives show how important change can be affected by purpose and how common people may have amazing results.

Purpose and mission are entwined in the modern world with solving some of the most urgent problems that humanity faces. Among the problems that need coordinated actions and a feeling of shared purpose are climate change, social injustice, and mental health crises. By matching personal goals with these more general societal issues, individuals may help to find answers that will have a significant effect. A job in sustainable technology development, for example, may be devoted to environmental protection, while a social justice advocate would work for laws that advance inclusiveness and equity.

One cannot stress the need of education in developing a feeling of purpose. It is the duty of educational institutions to promote emotional and moral as well as intellectual development. Students can find possible routes that fit with their sense of purpose if teachers encourage them to investigate their interests, values, and goals. People who follow this all-encompassing approach to schooling are better able to negotiate the intricacies of contemporary life and make significant contributions to society.

Moreover, the need for purpose-driven leadership is being acknowledged by the business world more and more. Companies that give social and environmental responsibility first priority and match their operations to a well-defined purpose typically have happier employees, loyal customers, and longer-term success. Because purpose-driven companies draw people who are enthusiastic about making a difference in the world, they are better able to innovate and adapt in a market that is changing quickly. This change within the business world toward purpose is a reflection of a larger cultural tendency to value effect and meaning more than just profit.

Equally significant to outside influences is the inward search for meaning and purpose. This means developing a growth mentality, resilience, and self-awareness through their ability to help people connect with their inner selves and clarify their goals and beliefs. Mindfulness techniques like journaling and meditation can support this process. Developing resilience by accepting obstacles and growing from setbacks also makes one more capable of tenaciously and determinedly pursuing their goal.

An additional important thing to think about is the meeting point of purpose and well-being. Strong sense of purpose, people tend to have better results for their mental and physical health, according to studies. Meaning and drive from purpose serve as a buffer against stress and hardship, improving general well-being. That purpose is frequently associated with life pleasure and longevity is not unexpected, therefore. People who are purposeful can not only have more happy lives but also improve the lives of people around them.

In a time of quick technical progress, the quest for meaning and purpose also occurs online. In this sense, there are both possibilities and problems with the emergence of social media, artificial intelligence, and other technical advancements. Technology may, on the one hand, make knowledge more widely shared, bring like-minded people together, and increase the effect of efforts with a purpose. If applied carelessly, though, it can also exacerbate existential anxiety and a sense of detachment. A major problem of the modern day is to strike a balance between the advantages of technology and the necessity for real human connection and purpose.

We need purpose and mission more and more as we negotiate the complexity of the twenty-first century. Individually and as a society, the search for meaning propels human development and promotes a feeling of fulfillment and belonging. A feeling of purpose helps people to contribute to the greater good and persevere in navigating the challenges of contemporary life. A more equitable, sustainable, and compassionate society is promised in this linked world when individual goals are in line with group issues.

Ultimately, today, more than ever, the world needs meaning and purpose. While advancing society and tackling global issues, these ideas provide people a sense of purpose and fulfillment. We may use purpose to improve everyone's future by encouraging self-awareness, resiliency, and a dedication to group well-being. Pursuing purpose and mission, whether via personal projects, educational programs, or business plans, is an essential part of life and has the power to effect significant and long-lasting change.

What You Can Be Paid For: Balancing financial stability with fulfillment

Many people struggle in the fast-changing economic environment of today to find rewarding work that also guarantees financial security. Many are reevaluating the conventional idea of a job as a means to an end as more individuals look for employment that offers more than simply a salary—they want a feeling of purpose and personal fulfillment. This paper looks at the difficulties of striking a balance between financial security and fulfillment, the changing definitions of success, and how to successfully combine the two in one's career.

Both individuals and families have a basic worry about financial stability. It gives access to basic necessities, including shelter, healthcare, education, and the odd recreational activity, therefore laying the groundwork for a safe and pleasant existence. The quest for financial security for many people starts with selecting a work path that offers development prospects and a consistent income. Because they pay well and are thought to offer employment stability, traditional professions like commerce, law, engineering, and medicine are frequently viewed as safe bets. But the way that jobs are changing—driven by globalization and technology breakthroughs—has expanded the range of viable professions and opened doors in previously unthinkable sectors.

Although having stable finances is important, the requirement of job contentment is becoming more and more acknowledged. In this view, fulfillment describes the inner contentment and feeling of direction that result from working on worthwhile projects that complement one's interests, values, and abilities. The need for human progress, connection, and contribution is the foundation of the quest for satisfaction. It is about locating happiness and meaning in one's work, which may have a big influence on general well-being and life satisfaction.

When people feel forced to choose between a lucrative career that lacks personal purpose and a meaningful career that might not provide the same degree of financial security, conflict between financial stability and fulfillment frequently results in cultures where financial riches and social standing are customarily used to gauge success, this problem is most noticeable. More individuals are, however, challenging this contradiction and looking for methods to include both aspects in their work as our definition of success changes.

One strategy to strike a balance between fulfillment and financial security is the idea of a "portfolio career." In a portfolio career, one pursues several professional positions and sources of income concurrently. This could be a mix of consultancy, part-time employment, freelancing, and side projects. Through professional diversification, people may work in jobs they enjoy personally and yet have financial security. This strategy lowers the chance of burnout and raises general job satisfaction by offering freedom and the chance to investigate several hobbies and talents.

One such tactic is to match one's professional path with sectors or positions that inherently offer fulfillment and financial security. Engage in the creative, sustainable development, and social entrepreneurship sectors, for instance, frequently enables people to engage in worthwhile and significant initiatives that also provide financial benefits. Furthermore, because they entail solving difficult challenges and advancing society, careers in technology and innovation may be profitable and satisfying. People may select jobs that meet their financial and personal demands by figuring out which industries speak to their beliefs and interests.

This equilibrium is mostly determined by education and ongoing learning. Learning new things could lead to jobs that provide both financial gain and personal satisfaction.

Finding out about developing areas like digital marketing, renewable energy, or artificial intelligence, for example, can open doors in fast-changing sectors. People wishing to change their occupations or improve their present positions to more closely match their objectives might find great value in professional development programs, online courses, and certifications.

Furthermore, there is growing recognition of the need for companies to create settings where staff members may attain financial security and contentment. Top talent is drawn to and retained by companies that put employee well-being first, provide chances for professional development, and share the same values as their staff. Programs for professional growth, flexible working schedules, and missions with a purpose may all improve employment happiness and engagement. Organizations may assist and empower their staff members to flourish both professionally and emotionally.

Personally, it takes knowledge of oneself and deliberate decision-making to strike a balance between financial security and fulfillment. It is choosing a job that fits with one's values, talents, and long-term objectives. Through their clarity and direction, reflective techniques like career coaching, mentoring, and journaling can help with this process. Furthermore, establishing reasonable financial objectives and creating a solid financial plan may relieve the strain of urgent money worries and enable people to work in long-term, meaningful jobs.

It is also critical to understand that the ratio of financial security to fulfillment may change with time. Priorities and job decisions can be influenced by life stages, personal situations, and outside influences. Early in a career, for example, financial security may be more important while people lay their groundwork and pay off debt. The emphasis could change as they have more experience and stability in their finances to locate more satisfying and in line with their interests. Navigating these changes and keeping a balanced approach need flexibility and openness to change.

Additionally intimately related to the larger idea of work-life balance is the idea of fulfillment at work. Long-term happiness and well-being need striking a good balance between work and personal obligations. This entails establishing limits, giving self-care first priority, and scheduling time for hobbies, relationships, and other non-work-related activities. One's personal health shouldn't suffer for a rewarding profession. Rather, it ought to support and improve these features, thereby enhancing a comprehensive feeling of well-being.

People now work and seek jobs in a far different way than they did in the past. Online platforms, the gig economy, and remote employment have given people new chances to strike a balance between fulfillment and financial security. For example, working remotely gives people freedom and flexibility in that they may plan their work hours around their personal lives. Pursuing side gigs and passion projects that can augment income and give one a sense of purpose is made possible by the gig economy. By facilitating networking, education, and teamwork, online platforms enable people to meet like-minded professionals and investigate a variety of professional options.

However, there are other difficulties with the digital era that need to be properly managed. Concerns that need attention are the blending of work and personal life, the necessity to be active all the time, and the possibility of employment instability in the gig economy. To take use of the advantages of the digital age while minimizing its drawbacks, one must acquire digital literacy, time management abilities, and a positive connection with technology.

In conclusion, striking a balance between financial security and fulfillment is a complex and ever-changing task that calls for a deliberate and deliberate strategy. It entails knowing oneself, one's talents, and one's objectives; it also entails looking into several job options and making wise choices that meet one's demands in terms of money and time. Those who embrace ideas like work-life balance, portfolio careers, and ongoing education may design financially stable and incredibly satisfying professional lives. By means of programs that give employee growth and well-being a top priority, organizations also significantly contribute to creating conditions that promote this balance. Achieving a fulfilling and meaningful job will still depend critically on the quest for a harmonic balance of financial security and fulfillment as the workplace changes.

CHAPTER III

Cultivating Passion and Mission

Techniques for discovering and nurturing passion
Discovering and sustaining one's passion is a path that intertwines with the pursuit of personal fulfillment and professional success. Passion is the driving energy that energizes and drives individuals, enabling them to pursue their goals with passion and determination. It is the aspect that converts work into a source of joy and personal progress. However, recognizing and nurturing passion is not always uncomplicated. This section covers different approaches that might help individuals uncover their actual interests and nurture them properly, assuring a life replete with purpose and happiness.

The first stage in developing passion is self-exploration and contemplation. Understanding oneself is vital in determining what actually stimulates and motivates an individual. This process begins with introspection when one assesses their interests, values, strengths, and experiences. Journaling may be a valuable tool in this regard. By frequently writing about everyday activities, thoughts, and feelings, individuals might obtain insights into repeating themes and patterns that suggest areas of great interest and potential passion. Questions such as "What activities make me lose track of time?" and "What subjects do I enjoy learning about?" might drive this introspective approach.

Another excellent strategy for discovering passion is to engage in varied activities. Exposure to new activities, locations, and cultures broadens one's viewpoint and helps unearth interests that may have stayed buried. Volunteering, traveling, taking workshops, and participating in community activities are practical methods to explore new interests. This experimenting period is vital as it allows individuals to explore their inclinations and measure their excitement for various hobbies. By venturing out of their comfort zones and also embracing new experiences, people might uncover passions they might not have explored otherwise.

Mentorship and networking also play key roles in the road to developing passion. Connecting with mentors, peers, and professionals who share similar interests may give useful insights and assistance. Conversations with experienced persons can expose numerous elements of a certain profession or activity, helping to define one's own interests. Networking events, professional groups, and internet forums are fantastic platforms for meeting mentors and like-minded individuals. These relationships not only give support and encouragement but also open doors to new possibilities and experiences that can further cultivate one's passion.

In addition to investigating outward experiences, it is necessary to listen to one's internal impulses. Pay attention to moments of delight, excitement, and satisfaction in daily life. These emotional responses are evidence of activities that resonate with one's actual interests. For instance, if a person gets a sense of thrill while solving complicated issues, it may signal a desire for analytical or scientific endeavors. Similarly, a great sense of fulfillment while helping others could suggest a desire for social work or community service. Recognizing and recognizing these emotional clues is vital in discovering and sustaining one's passion.

Once a possible interest is recognized, defining goals and building a strategy to pursue it consistently is vital. Goals give direction and inspiration, breaking down the road into small chunks. Start with tiny, realistic targets that generate momentum and confidence. When someone develops a love of writing, for example, they could start by committing to writing for half an hour every day. These little initiatives added together might eventually result in more audacious objectives like producing a book or publishing articles. A planned strategy guarantees constant advancement and supports dedication and concentration.

It takes ongoing education and skill improvement to cultivate enthusiasm. Competence and experience must be added to passion as it is insufficient on its alone. One can improve their knowledge and abilities in the selected area by taking classes, going to seminars, and pursuing certifications. Growing and learning not only makes one more involved in the activity but also creates new paths for success and discovery. For instance, a passion for cooking may be cultivated by studying different culinary methods, experimenting with new recipes, and understanding the science underlying food production.

Discovering and fostering passion also requires adopting a development mentality. Unlike fixed mindsets, growth mindsets hold that skills and abilities may be honed with commitment and effort. This viewpoint promotes resiliency, which motivates people to bear obstacles and disappointments. Retaining drive and enthusiasm requires accepting setbacks as teaching moments rather than as signs of inadequacy. Usually, not a straight line, the road to mastery entails getting over challenges and always trying to do better.

A long-term passion may also be sustained by self-care and balance. One may easily get so lost in their enthusiasm that they forget about other facets of life. Still, general well-being depends on striking a good balance between job, personal life, and leisure pursuits. Exercise, mindfulness, and also quality time with loved ones are among the activities that assist in replenishing and regenerating, therefore averting burnout. A well-rounded strategy guarantees that passion never turns into a cause of tension and fatigue but rather happiness and fulfillment.

Extend the satisfaction of one's desire to others. A feeling of community is formed, and the pleasure of the activity is increased when teaching, mentoring, or just exchanging experiences with like-minded people. An artist could, for example, get more fulfillment from teaching art or from showing in exhibits. In addition to confirming one's own knowledge and competence, imparting information and skills motivates and uplifts others, hence generating a positive feedback cycle.

The digital era and technology provide special chances to find and develop a passion. People may interact with people all over the world, get a plethora of knowledge, and display their skills thanks to social media and online platforms. People may make their passions known and supported by sharing them with a larger audience through blogs, podcasts, and YouTube channels. Skills may be developed and refined more easily with the accessible and reasonably priced access to learning materials offered by online courses and virtual seminars. Through the provision of previously unattainable networks and instruments, technology may greatly improve the process of discovering and fostering passion.

Periodically looking back on one's path and adjusting as necessary is also crucial. Time changes passion; it is never static. What inspires and thrills people now could not be the same in the future as their interests and circumstances shift. It is ensured that the pursuit of passion stays in line with personal development and fulfillment when one routinely evaluates their goals, progress, and contentment. A lifetime involvement with one's passions requires openness to change and a willingness to adapt.

The finding and developing of passion can also be influenced by cultural and social factors. It is essential to foster an atmosphere that appreciates and encourages a variety of interests and skills. People's goals and accomplishments are greatly influenced by their communities, jobs, and educational institutions. Through the promotion of an environment that values creativity, curiosity, and lifelong learning, society may enable people to follow their passions without worrying about criticism or failing.

One cannot stress the need for networking and mentoring in the identification and development of passion. Mentoring offers direction, encouragement, and a plethora of information from someone who has been where you are. A mentor could give advice, point up advantages and disadvantages, and provide perspective on how to overcome obstacles. Conversely, by interacting with a wide range of people who can motivate, work together, and assist, networking broadens one's perspectives. To create a network that fosters interest, go to industry events, join professional associations, and engage in internet forums.

A further crucial method for finding passion is to embrace curiosity and a readiness to investigate. The need to learn and explore is sparked by curiosity, which also results in new interests and maybe passions. Being playful and accepting is the result of giving oneself permission to explore without the need for instant accomplishment or mastery. Finding activities that really speak to people and arouse excitement requires this exploration stage. Someone could, for example, take up gardening out of interest and end up developing a deep love of horticulture and environmental sustainability.

Pursuing passion requires the development of a supportive attitude and constructive self-talk. Overcoming self-doubt and failure dread mostly requires believing in one's own skills and potential. An encouraging and like-minded environment, visualization exercises, and positive affirmations can all help to maintain a supportive attitude. This kind of thinking gives people the confidence and resiliency to pursue their passions, take chances, and meet obstacles head-on.

It is impossible to ignore how mindfulness and self-awareness help to find and develop passion. Because mindfulness techniques like deep breathing and meditation calm the mind and enable reflection, they improve self-awareness. Through the use of these techniques, people may better understand what is important to them. Engaging and present, mindfulness also improves the experience of joyful and fulfilling activities.

Finding passion takes practical exploration and practical experience. Even little experimentation yields priceless sensations and insights that theoretical study is unable to match. An interested party may, for example, check out a few instruments or take a few classes to find the one that most speaks to them. This useful method enables people to feel the subtleties and difficulties of many activities, which helps to pinpoint those that truly arouse interest and excitement.

Making the surroundings supportive and encouraging of passion is an essential part of cultivating it. This covers settings in real life, habits, and social networks that help one follow their passion. Creating a specific workstation, for example, creating a regular practice regimen and surrounding oneself with encouraging friends and family, may all help to foster enthusiasm. Passion may be more easily included in daily life when there is this kind of enabling infrastructure to maintain drive and dedication.

Another crucial factor is juggling enthusiasm with other obligations. Family, health, and financial security should not be sacrificed in order to follow and nurture one's passion. Getting things in balance guarantees that passion improves general well-being rather than turning into a cause of tension or disagreement. Achieving this balance mostly requires time management, realistic goal planning, and a comprehensive attitude to life.

Finally, finding and fostering passion is a complex process requiring introspection, a variety of experiences, ongoing education, and a supportive setting. In this process, mindfulness, practical experimentation, mentoring, and writing are all rather important. Using technology and networking possibilities, juggling passion with other obligations, and adopting a growth attitude all help one to follow and maintain passion. Finding and developing passion is ultimately a very personal and dynamic process that calls for a deliberate and deliberate approach. People may live lives richer in meaning, happiness, and fulfillment by taking this trip with curiosity, resiliency, and openness.

Overcoming obstacles and setbacks in pursuing passion

Following one's passion is an exciting, rewarding, and personally developing path. It is seldom easy or without difficulties, though. Setbacks and obstacles are given, and how people handle them frequently defines their level of success and happiness. This paper looks at the different challenges and disappointments one may run into when following their passion and offers solutions. Resilience development and an awareness of these obstacles can help people stick to their passions and reach their objectives.

A typical barrier to following a passion is the dread of failing. People might get immobilized by this dread and fail to take the required actions to achieve their objectives. One might become self-conscious and inactive because of an overpowering dread of failing or making mistakes. Overcoming this dread requires redefining failure as a teaching moment rather than a final destination. Taking up a growth mentality, which stresses the possibility of development and learning from setbacks, can assist people in seeing setbacks as worthwhile experiences that advance both their careers and personal lives. Gaining confidence and lowering the fear of failing can also come from identifying and celebrating little accomplishments.

Resources—time, money, and support—are another major barrier. Many people have interests that need either money or time commitments that they may not have because of other obligations like jobs, family, or school. To successfully manage this problem, one must create a practical strategy that takes into account present constraints and looks for innovative ways to distribute resources. This might entail creating a budget, looking for grants or scholarships, or figuring out how to include activities linked to passion in everyday life. Moreover, using internet forums, groups, and resources can offer free or very inexpensive access to information and assistance.

Passion can also be hampered by outside doubt and a lack of encouragement. One's enthusiasm may be misunderstood or even opposed by friends, family, or coworkers. It takes developing a strong sense of self-belief and locating a network of like-minded people who can provide support and direction to overcome this challenge. One may feel validated and at home by joining clubs, groups, or internet communities centered around their passion. Moreover, sometimes understanding and support may be developed by simply and forcefully explaining to doubters the value of one's passion and its effect on personal fulfillment.

An additional important difficulty is time management. It might be intimidating to juggle the quest of passion with obligations to one's family, job, and social life. Good time management techniques, like making plans, dividing goals into doable chores, and establishing clear priorities, can enable people to advance steadily without feeling overburdened. It is also critical to learn self-compassion and to accept that it is OK to change and take pauses as required. Realizing that pursuing passion is a marathon rather than a sprint helps keep one motivated over the long run and avoid burnout.

Many people struggle internally with self-doubt and impostor syndrome when following their hobbies. Anxiety and a lack of advancement can result from imposter syndrome, the sense of being a phony despite obvious achievement and skill. It takes awareness of and resistance to negative thought patterns and the development of a positive self-narrative to overcome self-doubt. Self-confidence may be increased by affirmations, mindfulness exercises, and asking peers or mentors for input. Reinforcing self-belief, recording accomplishments and thinking back on previous ones may also offer concrete proof of one's talents.

Exploring passion frequently means taking chances and negotiating uncertainty. Because of this innate ambiguity, one may hesitate or second-guess. Develop a tolerance for ambiguity and concentrate on controllable elements in order to handle uncertainty. People who are flexible in their aims, adaptive, and solution-oriented may remain resilient in the face of uncertainty. Accepting change as a chance for development as opposed to danger can also encourage a proactive strategy for getting over challenges.

One typical obstacle that might prevent one from following their passion is procrastinating. It may be harmful to objectives to put off doing things, particularly those that are difficult or outside of one's comfort zone. Understanding the root reasons for procrastination, including perfectionism, lack of enthusiasm, or fear of failing, is necessary to overcome it. Methods that assist in boosting productivity include the Pomodoro Technique, which divides work into brief, concentrated intervals and establishes deadlines. Focus and productivity may also be increased by reducing distractions and establishing a comfortable work environment.

Many people find that following their hobbies is hampered by financial volatility, particularly in professions that cannot provide a steady or considerable salary. It is critical to handle this problem pragmatically, balancing financial obligations with enthusiasm. This might include keeping up part-time employment while pursuing passion projects, creating many sources of income, or saving money preparatory to making significant life changes.

Additionally able to offer stability and lessen stress associated with financial uncertainty are financial planning, budgeting, and consulting financial consultants.

Both mental and physical health problems could be major obstacles in the way of pursuing enthusiasm. One may not be able to participate completely in things they are enthusiastic about if they have chronic diseases, injuries, or mental health issues. It is essential to give health and well-being first priority via frequent exercise, healthy eating, enough sleep, and getting expert assistance when needed. Finding strategies to modify passion-related activities to one's physical and mental capacities and building a supportive atmosphere that meets health requirements can help maintain interest and development.

Additionally impeding the pursuit of passion are social and cultural obstacles. People might run into challenges from systematic prejudices, cultural standards, and societal expectations, especially those from underprivileged groups. It takes self-advocacy, allying with others, and making use of chances and resources to overcome these obstacles. Taking up activism and spreading knowledge of these problems can also help to bring about more general institutional adjustments that encourage everyone to follow their passion. Navigating social and cultural obstacles demands developing resilience and a solid support system.

A further typical setback is the impression of immobility or lack of advancement. Sometimes, passion projects reach a standstill when advancement appears to be sluggish or nonexistent. This could make one frustrated and demoralized. To go above this, one must often reevaluate objectives, mark little accomplishments, and look for fresh challenges that can stoke excitement. To break through stagnation, network with people in your industry, go to seminars, or look for mentoring. Keeping an open mind and being receptive to fresh learning chances will help keep drive and momentum high.

Juggling several interests might be difficult as well. Some people have many hobbies and find it difficult to concentrate on just one at a time. This can cause work to be dispersed and no appreciable advancement in any one area. To handle this, one must rank passions according to present objectives and situations. Effective management of several interests may be achieved by creating a systematic strategy that gives each passion specific time and resources while allowing for flexibility to change as required. More significant and long-lasting advancement might result from acknowledging that it might not be feasible to follow all passions at once and from carefully choosing where to focus time and effort.

The need for self-care and relaxation is one sometimes disregarded component of conquering challenges in following passion. Burnout from overextending oneself without getting enough sleep can sap motivation and reduce output. Keeping one's energy and attention requires include frequent pauses, leisure activities, and self-care routines. Techniques for mindfulness and relaxation, including yoga, meditation, or time spent in the outdoors, can lower stress and improve general well-being. It takes awareness of the warning indicators of burnout and prompt action to deal with it in order to maintain sustained involvement with one's interest.

One more way to go over challenges is to have a resilient and persistent attitude. Being resilient is being able to overcome obstacles and keep a good attitude. By use of techniques like cognitive restructuring—which entails reversing negative beliefs into positive ones—and creating coping mechanisms for stress and hardship, resilience may be developed. Having encouraging and upbeat people in one's life might also help one develop a resilient attitude. Knowing that challenges are a normal aspect of every worthwhile endeavor and seeing them as chances for personal development helps keep one motivated and persistent.

Seeking expert advice, such as coaching or job counseling, may be quite helpful in getting beyond challenges and disappointments. Professional coaches and counselors may provide unbiased viewpoints, doable guidance, and plans catered to specific requirements and objectives. They can help define reasonable objectives, pinpoint areas of strength and progress, and create doable strategies to get there. Putting money into professional advice may pay off, especially in times of change or when faced with big problems that call for specific knowledge.

Overcoming challenges and disappointments also need insight and reflection. Time spent in introspection on one's path, obstacles encountered, and lessons discovered can yield insightful information. Journaling or meditation are two reflective methods that can assist people in sorting through their experiences, seeing trends, and making wise choices for the future. Through introspection, people become more self-aware and grow personally, which helps them to face obstacles with more assurance and direction.

Overcoming challenges pertaining to competence and experience requires laying a solid basis of knowledge and abilities. One can improve their skills and gain confidence in following passion-related activities via ongoing education and professional growth. This can include signing up for classes, going to workshops, going for certificates, or studying on your own via books, articles, and internet resources. Having a strong skill set not only increases performance but also creates new chances and routes to follow passions.

And last, getting beyond challenges and disappointments requires keeping a long-term perspective. Many times, passion projects are bumpy, lifetime journeys. Long-term vision helps keep one motivated and resilient amid trying circumstances. Having both long- and short-term goals and then routinely evaluating and changing them as necessary guarantees that the larger vision is being reached. The drive to go over challenges can be found in realizing that failures are fleeting and that success will eventually come via perseverance and effort.

Finally, pursuing passion is a complex undertaking that calls for tenacity, flexibility, and initiative to overcome challenges and disappointments. People may travel their pathways with more confidence and resolve if they handle internal issues like self-doubt, procrastination, and fear of failing, as well as external ones like lack of resources, social barriers, and time limits. The pursuit of passion is sustained in large part by techniques including cultivating a growth mindset, using support networks, time management that works, lifelong learning, and self-care. A life that is meaningful and purposeful is ensured when people embrace failures as chances for personal development and keep a long-term outlook.

Defining one's mission and purpose in life

Identifying one's life's goal and purpose is a serious and very personal endeavor. It is knowing who we are, what we value, and what we hope to accomplish in our lifetime. Many times, this journey is characterized by reflection, investigation, and, occasionally, a great deal of doubt. For one to live a happy and meaningful life, one must first identify and articulate their mission and purpose. This section looks at all the different facets of this trip and provides advice and techniques to assist people in dealing with this significant part of life.

Determining one's mission and purpose starts with self-awareness. Finding out who one is is essential to knowing what is important in life. Explored are one's passions, values, interests, and strengths. One helpful instrument in this process is introspection. Frequent self-reflection through activities like writing, meditation, or reflective walks can help one understand their own goals and driving forces better. Inquiring of oneself, "What makes me happy?" This introspective approach might be directed by the questions, "What am I naturally good at?" and "What values are most important to me?" By means of such reflection, people start to identify the fundamental components that define their goals and objectives.

Determining a goal and purpose requires first knowing one's values. The guiding principles that direct our decisions and deeds are our values. These are the ideals we have of ourselves and the traits we think are significant in life. Finding and ranking these values provides a precise structure for choosing and achieving objectives. If one respects compassion and assists others, for example, their goal and purpose may be to work in social services, healthcare, or community development. Achieving a goal that is in line with strongly held beliefs guarantees authenticity and fulfillment of the endeavor.

Another important part of this trip is discovering hobbies and passions. The things that excite and arouse enthusiasm are called passions. They are frequently clues as to one's actual calling. To find their interests, people should explore new things, have a variety of experiences, and consider what makes them feel most alive. Traveling, volunteering, going to seminars, and following interests may all provide one important insight into their true passions. With time, trends and recurrent motifs show possible places where one's goal and purpose may be.

Determining one's mission and purpose also requires an awareness of one's own abilities and talents. These are the unavoidable talents and abilities of a person. It takes awareness of and use of these advantages to develop a worthwhile and realistic purpose. Assessments of strengths, personality types, and outside comments can all give important information about a person's special talents. After they are recognized, these advantages might be included into the goal to make sure the endeavor is in line with one's strongest suit.

Determining and following one's mission and purpose practically starts with setting objectives. As they divide the larger task into doable steps, goals give direction and a feeling of purpose. Developing SMART goals—specific, measurable, realistic, relevant, and time-bound—is essential to effective goal setting. This methodical technique guarantees consistent advancement toward the goal by helping to keep desire and attention high. It is equally crucial to be adaptable and willing to change objectives as necessary. Life is dynamic; hence, finding one's purpose may call for flexibility and resiliency.

One cannot stress the need for mentoring and direction on this path. Mentors provide their own experiences as well as insightful advice, encouragement, and viewpoints. They may point up blind areas, give helpful criticism, and support you through trying times. Finding and following one's mission may be much aided by seeking mentoring from those who have accomplished comparable things or who have similar ideals. Moreover, being in the company of encouraging people who share your values produces a supportive atmosphere that promotes development.

A critical component of this path is accepting failure and growing from disappointments. One must frequently overcome barriers and difficulties on the rarely straight route to establishing and realizing their goal and purpose. Resilience and drive need to be maintained by seeing setbacks as teaching moments rather than final conclusions. Every disappointment teaches important lessons that advance oneself and help one make wiser choices. A growth mentality, which stresses that people may grow and learn via work and tenacity, can enable them to approach obstacles with optimism and initiative.

Pursuing a meaningful cause requires ongoing education and self-improvement. People who study throughout their lives are certain to be flexible and receptive to fresh chances and discoveries. This might be self-directed study through books, internet courses, and experiential activities, or formal education and professional growth. Curious and dedicated to personal development not only improves abilities and knowledge but also maintains the path to achieving one's goal interesting and dynamic. Taking up an attitude of ongoing development guarantees that the search for purpose changes and stays in line with one's interests and circumstances.

Another crucial factor is juggling personal and business life. Relationships, health, and general well-being should not suffer in the name of pursuing a goal. Setting limits, giving self-care first priority, and making sure that pursuing one's goal coexists peacefully with other obligations and interests are all part of achieving balance. Over time, people may continue their enthusiasm and dedication because of this all-encompassing strategy, which guarantees ongoing inspiration and avoids burnout. A sustained quest for meaning depends on realizing that fulfillment arises from a well-rounded existence where all aspects are nourished.

The process of determining one's goal and purpose may be much improved by including mindfulness and presence. A sense of presence and awareness is developed via mindfulness exercises like meditation, deep breathing, and mindful walking. People can have closer relationships with both their inner selves and the outside world when they are totally present in each moment. This increased awareness can provide important insights into what is important, which can help to focus and define their objective. Apart from that, mindfulness may lower stress and improve general well-being, which facilitates a more deliberate and concentrated search for purpose.

To remain in line with the goal, one must often consider their experiences and development. Frequent introspection offers the chance to evaluate what is and is not functioning, as well as how personal development is developing. This might be scheduling time specifically for introspection through writing, talking with mentors, or contemplative activities. Investigative queries like "What have I learned?" "How have I grown?" and "What adjustments do I need to make?" help direct this process. The quest for purpose is kept dynamic and sensitive to evolving conditions and insights by this regular assessment.

Contributing to something bigger than oneself is another critical component of identifying one's mission and purpose. The effect one has on other people and the world is frequently intimately related to a feeling of purpose. Participating in things that advance the environment, society, or community may give one a great feeling of purpose and fulfillment. This may be anything from lobbying to charity to volunteer work to any endeavors meant to change the world. Knowing how one's work fits into the greater fabric of the human experience may motivate and keep one going, leaving a legacy of constructive change.

One's mission and purpose can be defined in part via spirituality and philosophical study. Examining spiritual or philosophical viewpoints could help one understand existence, human values, and the purpose of life more deeply. Studying, practicing, or conversing with people from several spiritual or philosophical traditions could help one better comprehend and guide their search for meaning. This investigation can provide a wider background for individual experiences and goals, therefore enabling one to place their purpose within a more comprehensive framework of significance and interconnectedness.

Determining one's goal and purpose requires creativity and self-expression. When people express themselves creatively—through writing, music, art, or other means—they are able to investigate and communicate their inner experiences and goals. Ingenuity, problem-solving, and the capacity to see new opportunities are all promoted by creativity. It offers a potent platform for expressing one's own voice and viewpoint, therefore advancing knowledge of oneself and one's purpose. Accepting inventiveness as a part of the process guarantees that the search for meaning never becomes old or boring.

Empathy and emotional intelligence are critical abilities for negotiating the route of identifying and realizing one's purpose. Relationships and decision-making are improved when one is aware of and in control of their own emotions as well as those of others. Developing emotional intelligence calls for motivation, empathy, self-control, self-awareness, and social skills. These abilities enable productive cooperation, communication, and settlement of conflicts—all of which are essential for carrying out any task requiring human contact. Because it links one's own goals with the welfare of others, developing empathy and compassion also helps one feel more connected to their mission.

Refinement and validation of one's goal and purpose need practical experience and active participation. Taking part in practical tasks linked to one's interests and objectives yields concrete information and criticism. This can include project partnerships, volunteer activities, internships, or business endeavors. People who have practical experience are better able to challenge their presumptions, acquire essential abilities, and establish a successful record. It also offers chances to connect with colleagues and experts in the industry, thereby being exposed to other viewpoints and best practices. Engaging in real life helps to close the gap between theoretical goals and actual reality, therefore guaranteeing that one's purpose is realistic and doable.

Finally, the path to discovering one's mission and purpose requires one to stay curious and receptive. Exploration, education, and the openness to challenge presumptions and welcome novel concepts are all fueled by curiosity. People who are open-minded can adjust to new situations and develop interests. It encourages awe and discovery, which keeps the path toward purpose interesting and dynamic. To cultivate curiosity is to look for novel experiences, pose questions, and be open to unanticipated changes and revelations. A mind that is open and inquisitive guarantees that the search for meaning will always be an exciting and changing journey.

Finally, discovering one's passion, values, and practical goals are all part of the complex and extremely personal process of defining one's mission and purpose in life. It means negotiating obstacles both inside and outside of oneself, looking for advice and mentorship, accepting lifelong learning and development, and keeping a calm and balanced attitude. The trip is made much more enjoyable by emotional intelligence, inventiveness, real-world experience, and curiosity. Through the integration of these components, people may find and follow a genuine, rewarding, and significant mission that will result in a meaningful and purposeful existence.

Aligning daily actions with a greater mission

Practice that makes ambitions abstract into concrete is matching everyday activities with a larger purpose. This alignment guarantees that every day significantly advances the main objectives of life, giving one direction, fulfillment, and a feeling of purpose. To get this alignment, though, calls for self-awareness, discipline, and intention. The significance, difficulties, and methods for achieving and sustaining this alignment are examined in this section, along with the need to coordinate everyday activities with a larger goal.

Knowing that little, regular acts add up to big results over time is the foundation of matching everyday activities with a larger goal. This theory, sometimes expressed as "the compound effect," highlights how daily decisions taken together may have a significant influence on a person's life. It is so important to understand that every choice and deed, no matter how little, either advances or detracts from one's larger goal. By fostering a proactive attitude, this knowledge motivates people to make thoughtful decisions that advance their long-term objectives.

The first and most important step in coordinating everyday activities with a larger goal is to define that goal precisely. This is realizing one's main values, goals, and the differences one wants to have. Every day, decision-making is guided by a well-defined mission, which also offers a clear sense of direction. One useful instrument in this process might be writing a personal purpose statement. This statement provides a continual reminder of what is really important by briefly summarizing one's basic principles, purpose, and objectives. It could be a benchmark for determining if day-to-day activities are in line with more general goals.

Setting precise, practical goals that divide the more complex mission into doable activities comes next once the mission has been well defined. These should be SMART goals—specific, measurable, attainable, relevant, and time-bound. By establishing SMART objectives, one may be confident that the larger purpose is converted into doable actions that can be included in regular activities. If one wants to improve their health and well-being, for instance, establishing certain objectives like working out for half an hour every day, eating a healthy diet, and also getting enough sleep may help them take concrete steps in that direction.

Managing your time well is essential to coordinating everyday activities with a bigger goal. Time management done well includes setting priorities for jobs that advance long-term objectives and reducing diversions and pointless activity. Actions most in line with one's objective can be prioritized with the use of techniques like the Eisenhower Matrix, which ranks jobs according to urgency and priority. These priorities are also regularly addressed if a planned daily schedule is created that sets out time for mission-related tasks. Furthermore, improving attention and productivity is time blocking, which sets aside particular timeslots for particular activities.

Sustaining discipline and consistency is another critical component. Although it is simple to become excited and inspired about a purpose at first, long-term maintenance of this enthusiasm calls for discipline. Establishing routines and behaviors that advance the goal might assist in preserving consistency. Setting up a morning routine, for example, with exercises, meditation, or day-to-day preparation, could help to build a good attitude and strengthen connection with one's purpose. In a similar vein, a nightly ritual that includes thinking back on the day's achievements and making plans for the next helps keep one focused and moving forward.

It takes mindfulness and self-awareness to make sure that everyday activities continue to be in line with a bigger purpose. Being totally present in the present moment, or mindful, helps one to see if present activities advance or undermine long-term objectives. Techniques for developing this awareness include meditation, deep breathing, and careful observation. Maintaining alignment may be accomplished by routinely checking in with oneself and posing thoughtful questions like "Is this action moving me closer to my mission?" or "How does this activity align with my values?" A further aspect of self-awareness is identifying and changing any patterns or actions that might be impeding development.

Getting over roadblocks and diversions is a big part of matching everyday activities to a bigger goal. Unexpected things happen, conflicting needs arise, and distractions abound that can throw off concentration and dedication in life. To keep alignment plans to handle these obstacles must be developed. Boundaries may be established in this way, including allocating particular periods for concentrated work and reducing disruptions. It might also need to gain the flexibility and resilience to overcome obstacles and go on. Both socially and physically, creating a supportive atmosphere can assist in lessening distractions and strengthen dedication to the goal.

Daily activities must be kept in line with the larger goal by regular introspection and evaluation. This is ensuring that plans, progress, and goals are still applicable and successful by routinely evaluating them. Journaling, self-evaluation activities, and conversations with peers and mentors are just a few ways that reflection could manifest. Inquiring as to "What have I accomplished so far?" "What obstacles have I faced?" and "What changes must I make?" might offer insightful information and direct future behavior. Frequent introspection preserves a flexible and adaptable attitude to coordinating everyday activities with the larger purpose.

A further effective instrument for preserving alignment is accountability. One feels more responsible and supported when one shares their mission and objectives with reliable friends, family, or mentors. Continually informing these people of your achievements and difficulties might inspire and motivate them. Partners in accountability may applaud accomplishments, provide helpful criticism, and guide through challenges. Assembling a network of support and a feeling of accountability and common purpose may also result from joining communities or groups with similar objectives.

It takes celebration of little accomplishments and turning points to keep motivation high and alignment strong. No matter how little an accomplishment, acknowledging and enjoying it gives one a sense of success and advancement. It makes the trip more fulfilling and pleasurable by reiterating the relationship between everyday activities and the larger goal. Celebrations may be anything from giving oneself a favorite pastime to doing, telling people about accomplishments, or just pausing to acknowledge one's own growth. This exercise feeds ongoing dedication to the goal and helps to keep one optimistic.

Complementing everyday activities with a larger goal also calls for ongoing education and development. People who follow their objective come into fresh obstacles, chances, and realizations that advance their careers and personal lives. Taking on an attitude of lifelong learning guarantees that one is flexible and receptive to fresh opportunities. This might entail going for fresh experiences, knowledge, and abilities via self-directed learning, professional development, or formal school. It helps one to navigate the path and remain in line with the goal of being inquisitive and proactive in personal development.

It takes balancing short- and long-term viewpoints to match everyday activities to a larger purpose. While it is critical to concentrate on short-term objectives and chores, keeping a long-term perspective guarantees that these activities support the larger purpose. This equilibrium means being adaptable and receptive to changing conditions while routinely reviewing and restating one's mission and long-term objectives. It also means realizing that, typically, progress toward a bigger goal is slow and incremental, needing endurance and patience. Combining these viewpoints keeps one motivated and guarantees that everyday activities stay in line with long-term goals.

For ongoing alignment, self-care and well-being must be included in the quest for a bigger goal. Maintaining physical, mental, and emotional health requires self-care since the road to completing a purpose can be rigorous and difficult. Regular exercise, good food, enough sleep, and relaxation methods all promote general health and improve resilience and focus. Nurturing connections and doing happy, relaxing things can help to maintain balance and avoid burnout. Understanding that pursuing a cause requires self-care guarantees one to stay inspired and driven.

Aligning everyday activities with a larger goal inevitably requires adjustment to change and uncertainty. Because life is dynamic, things could change out of the blue, needing changes to plans and tactics. For alignment to endure, resilience and flexibility development are essential. This means being receptive to new chances, recvaluating plans and objectives as needed, and being prepared to change course as needed. Accepting change as an inevitable aspect of the trip promotes a proactive and strong attitude that guarantees one stay in line with the main goal in spite of obstacles and doubts.

For alignment and ongoing growth, feedback and experience learning must be included. Experiences, mentors, peers, or self-evaluation can offer insightful information about what is and is not working. It helps one to improve plans and deeds to be open to criticism and see it as a chance for improvement. Every experience guarantees that it advances and aligns by teaching from both triumphs and mistakes. This feedback and learning process is iterative, promotes a culture of ongoing development, and guarantees that everyday activities stay in line with the overall objective.

One cannot stress the importance of passion and internal drive in coordinating everyday activities with a larger purpose. The motivation and excitement required to maintain a commitment to long-term objectives are supplied by passion. Extrinsic motivation depends on outside incentives; intrinsic motivation originates from the inside and is motivated by personal beliefs and interests. Developing passion and intrinsic motivation means doing things that align with your interests and beliefs, finding purpose in the work, and appreciating the intangible benefits of development. This inner motivation keeps things going and makes sure that everyday activities stay in line with the larger goal.

At last, developing a feeling of direction and significance in day-to-day activities improves connection with the larger goal. A deep sense of contentment and also satisfaction that comes from purpose and significance makes the trip meaningful and fulfilling. This is knowing how one's acts affect and matter for oneself and other people. One feels more purposeful and meaningful when everyday activities are related to the larger mission and acknowledged for their contribution to long-term objectives. By improving motivation and dedication, this viewpoint makes sure that everyday activities are in line with and advance the larger goal.

Finally, it is a complex and dynamic process that calls for self-awareness, discipline, and intentionality to match everyday activities with a larger purpose. It entails establishing specific objectives, time management techniques, consistency and discipline, mindfulness and self-awareness cultivation, and a clear definition of the purpose. Essential tactics on this path are overcoming challenges, routine introspection and evaluation, accountability, recognizing accomplishments, ongoing education, balancing viewpoints, integrating self-care, adjusting to change, incorporating feedback, and fostering passion and intrinsic motivation. Adopting these techniques will help people make sure that their everyday activities significantly advance their long-term objectives, which will result in a happy and meaningful existence.

CHAPTER IV

Embracing Vocation and Profession

Exploring the concept of vocation and meaningful work

A core part of the human experience, the ideas of vocation and meaningful employment reflect our innate need to find meaning and purpose in our everyday actions. From the Latin "vocare," which means "to call," the term "vocation" has long meant a heavenly call to a life of religion. But now days, it has developed to include a wider range of callings, including different careers and life paths that people are drawn to. Conversely, fulfilling, significant, and in line with one's values and interests job is referred to as meaningful work. This study examines the psychological and intellectual foundations of these ideas, their historical development, and their relevance in the workplace of today.

Avocation was historically mostly connected to religious activities. A life devoted to God, either in the walls of a monastery or as a member of the clergy, was seen in the medieval Christian tradition as a divine invitation. Early Christian thinkers like Augustine and Thomas Aquinas, whose emphasis on the sanctity of committing one's life to spiritual activities, greatly impacted this perspective. But a big change in how people saw vocation came with the Protestant Reformation of the 16th century, especially with the writings of Martin Luther and John Calvin. Not simply religious or clerical labor, they suggested, may be viewed as a calling from God in any kind of employment. This democratization of vocation proposed that common jobs—farming, crafts, or teaching, for example—were as significant in God's eyes and may be followed with a feeling of divine mission.

Vocation as a notion changed much more as nations moved from rural to industrialized economies. The contemporary era's advent of capitalism and emphasis on individuality changed the emphasis from divine calling to personal satisfaction and social contribution. Max Weber contended in his influential book "The Protestant Ethic and the Spirit of Capitalism," that by encouraging virtues like thrift, discipline, and hard effort, the Protestant work ethic had a major impact on the growth of capitalism. Weber proposed that meaningful labor may be found in many professional fields, not only in religious life, and that the sense of calling in one's job became a driving force behind economic production and personal accomplishment.

For many people these days, finding meaningful job has taken front stage. What meaningful work is now being reevaluated in light of the quick changes in the employment market, globalization, and technical breakthroughs. For many, aspects of meaningful employment include personal development, the chance to have a good influence, compatibility with personal beliefs, and a feeling of community and connection with others. Theories of psychology, including self-determination theory (SDT), provide light on the innate incentives that propel people toward fulfilling careers. According to SDT people are driven by their need for relatedness, competence, and autonomy. When these demands are satisfied at work, people are more inclined to find their jobs to be relevant and satisfying.

Additionally useful viewpoints are offered by the philosophical investigation of meaningful labor. Existentialist philosophers like Viktor Frankl and Jean-Paul Sartre stress the need of personal choice and the quest for meaning in order to build a meaningful life. Sartre's idea of "existence precedes essence" implies that people must make their own meaning by their decisions and deeds, not by depending on predestined goals. Frankl emphasizes in his book "Man's Search for Meaning," the need of finding meaning even in the face of hardship and pain. A basic human desire, Frankl believed that labor may provide a strong sense of purpose when it is in line with one's ideals and advances a cause bigger than oneself.

Organizations are realizing more and more in the contemporary workplace how crucial it is to create meaningful work environments. Employers that put employee well-being first, provide chances for professional growth, and foster a feeling of community and purpose typically have happier and more engaged staff. Research indicates that motivated, productive, and loyal workers are those who feel their jobs important. Furthermore, higher mental health outcomes—which lower the chance of burnout and raise general well-being—are associated with meaningful employment.

Many tactics are needed to establish a culture of meaningful work. First of all, companies may concentrate on job design, making sure that positions are set up to offer challenge, autonomy, and chances to use skills. Furthermore contributing to the sense of purpose is job crafting, which allows workers to customize their duties and responsibilities to better suit their interests and skills. Second, creating a purposeful culture is mostly the responsibility of the leadership. Employees might feel a sense of purpose and belonging from leaders who clear up their vision, motivate and encourage their colleagues, and exhibit a dedication to moral principles.

It's also critical to promote a feeling of camaraderie and connection at work. When workers feel appreciated and linked to their coworkers, collaborative work settings can improve general feeling of purpose and fulfillment.

Through promoting a balance between work and personal life and understanding that meaningful work is a component of a full life, organizations may also help employees discover purpose. This all-encompassing strategy recognizes that people get meaning from a variety of sources, such as family, interests, and community service, and that promoting a good work-life balance may improve general well-being.

Finding a calling and fulfilling career is not without difficulties. People may encounter constraints and uncertainties in a fast evolving labor market that impede their quest of fulfilling careers. Stress can be caused and the search for satisfying employment hampered by economic issues, job instability, and the necessity to learn new skills and technology. Furthermore, ideas of what meaningful work is can be shaped by society expectations and cultural conventions, which occasionally push people along routes that are not really in line with their interests and ideals.

It takes introspection and investigation for people to overcome these obstacles. Finding possible professional routes that create a feeling of meaning and purpose may be made easier by knowing one's values, talents, and hobbies. Additionally useful tools for helping people define their objectives and negotiate the intricacies of the job market are career counseling and mentoring. Moreover, in a changing workplace, a readiness to change and welcome lifelong learning is essential as it enables people to always match their interests and talents with new chances.

In summary, the ideas of vocation and meaningful employment are fundamental to the human experience and represent our natural need for meaning and purpose. Historically based in religious traditions, these ideas have developed to include a more comprehensive view of labor as a source of both social and personal meaning. Understanding the values and reasons that propel people toward meaningful work, psychological and philosophical viewpoints emphasize the value of autonomy, competence, and relatedness. In the contemporary office, creating a culture of meaningful work requires careful job design, encouraging leadership, and a feeling of community. By introspection, mentoring, and flexibility, people may successfully negotiate the quest for vocation and meaningful employment despite the obstacles presented by a fast evolving labor market. In the end, the search for purposeful and happy life revolves around the dynamic and continuous adventure of finding meaningful job.

Assessing skills to find a fulfilling vocation

It takes self-discovery, talent evaluation, and real-world application to find a meaningful career. A vocation goes beyond simple job happiness to include a greater feeling of direction and compatibility with one's interests and ideals. Finding a career that fulfills one is dependent on doing a comprehensive evaluation of their abilities and realizing how they may be used in the working world. This paper explores the techniques and approaches for evaluating talents in order to choose a career that is fulfilling, enlightening, and in line with one's life objectives.

This process starts with reflection and self-awareness. Fundamentally important is knowing who you are, what motivates you, and where your talents are. You may start this self-evaluation with a number of contemplative exercises. Keeping a diary is a great way to monitor your ideas, successes, and setbacks over time and to get insights on trends that might highlight your hobbies and main skills. By creating a setting of introspective clarity and emotional equilibrium, meditation and mindfulness techniques can contribute to the development of a clearer sense of self. A deeper insight into what really interests and drives you is made possible by these techniques.

Structured skills assessment comes next when a basic degree of self-awareness is achieved. Technical and quantitative hard skills and interpersonal, frequently more subjective soft skills are the two main categories into which skills fall. Soft talents include communication, leadership, problem-solving, and emotional intelligence; hard skills include things like technical know-how, linguistic ability, or certain credentials. Finding a profession that is both appropriate and satisfying requires a fair assessment of both skill sets.

Using career aptitude tests and self-assessment tools is one efficient way to evaluate talents. StrengthsFinder, the Holland Code, and the Myers-Briggs Type Indicator (MBTI) are just a few of the tools that may provide you with important information about your personality, talents, and possible professional routes. One personality type tool that helps determine how you interact with the environment and make decisions is the MBTI. StrengthsFinder helps you pinpoint your strongest abilities for use in your career. With its useful guidance to professions that fit your natural inclinations, the Holland Code combines your interests and talents with possible work settings.

Strengths, Weaknesses, Opportunities, and also Threats, or SWOT analysis, may also provide you with a thorough picture of your abilities in relation to your professional goals. Finding your advantages and disadvantages can help you to better determine which abilities are already well-developed and which ones may need more work. Making educated choices regarding future career paths might be facilitated by identifying possibilities in your present professional route and possible obstacles to your advancement.

Invaluable tools in the skills evaluation process are also peer feedback and mentoring. Colleagues, managers, and mentors may provide an outside viewpoint on your strengths and places for development. Particularly, mentors can assist you in negotiating the challenges of professional growth by offering advice based on their own experiences and expertise. Talking honestly and constructively with reliable people on a regular basis may reveal weaknesses and draw attention to talents you would not otherwise see.

Evaluation of talents and selection of a rewarding career depends heavily on practical experience and experimentation. Practical changes to put your abilities to the test in practical situations include internships, volunteer work, part-time jobs, and freelancing ventures. These encounters not only help you hone your abilities but also make it more evident what kinds of jobs and work settings appeal to you. Taking on a variety of professional experiences can highlight unanticipated talents and interests and point you in the direction of a career that fits your skills and interests.

Evaluation of talents and career contentment depend heavily on educational goals and ongoing education. Taking classes, going to seminars, and going for credentials in your field of interest may all help you hone and confirm your abilities. Online learning possibilities abound and are reasonably priced on several sites, including Coursera, Udemy, and LinkedIn Learning. These educational opportunities improve your abilities and show a dedication to both professional and personal development, which increases your appeal to employers.

Identifying a rewarding career and evaluating talents also need networking. Developing a network of experts in the area you want to work in might reveal information about career prospects, industry trends, and the abilities needed to succeed. Joining trade groups, going to industry conferences, and networking events are all good methods to meet like-minded people and learn useful knowledge. Furthermore, improving your abilities and career prospects are joint initiatives and mentoring possibilities that might result from networking.

Apart from networking, using internet resources and technologies can facilitate the process of talent evaluation. With sites like LinkedIn, you can build a professional profile that highlights your accomplishments, experiences, and talents. Update your profile often, and ask coworkers for recommendations to assist prospective employers in verifying your qualifications. Furthermore, acting as dynamic displays of your work, online portfolios, and personal websites may offer concrete proof of your skills and achievements.

A successful career requires both self-promotion and personal branding. In a cutthroat employment market, building a personal brand that fairly captures your abilities, beliefs, and career goals may help set you apart.

This includes putting together an appealing LinkedIn profile, a polished CV, and a regular online presence as part of a coherent story surrounding your professional identity. By enabling you to present your special value offer to possible clients, employers, and partners, personal branding raises your chances of landing a job that fits your interests and talents.

Finding a rewarding career and evaluating talents also need a readiness to change and grow. The employment market is dynamic and new chances frequently materialize in reaction to new technology and trends. It can improve your flexibility and resilience to keep up with changes in the sector and to be willing to learn new skills. This preventive strategy makes sure you stay competitive and current in your chosen area, which raises the possibility of discovering a career that will eventually provide you with satisfaction.

Finding a rewarding career requires resilience and tenacity, among other important traits. Career search and talent assessment may be difficult processes with many roadblocks and disappointments. Long-term success requires keeping a good attitude and seeing setbacks as chances to improve. Creating resilience is learning stress-management techniques, asking peers and mentors for help, and keeping a good work-life balance.

Matching your work with your moral and ethical beliefs is another essential component in discovering a rewarding profession. Deeper happiness and a feeling of purpose are probably to be found in a career that aligns with your basic principles and benefits society. Making well-informed choices may be achieved by thinking about your beliefs and how they relate to possible professional routes. If sustainability, for example, is a fundamental goal, working in the environmental sciences or green technology could be especially rewarding. In the same vein, jobs in social work, education, or healthcare can be more in line with your ideals if helping others is your top goal.

Finding a rewarding career also depends critically on integrating work-life balance. All around well-being depends on a career that enables a good balance between professional and personal obligations. It's critical to evaluate possible careers for their capacity to offer possibility for personal development, flexibility, and reasonable stress levels. Your personal and lifestyle choices as well as your professional ambitions should be supported by a rewarding career.

Professional development courses and mentoring may be quite helpful in guiding people toward achieving success in a rewarding career. Companies that provide tools for professional growth, leadership development, and organized mentoring programs give staff members looking to progress in their jobs important assistance. Engaging in these courses may improve your abilities, expand your network of professionals, and offer direction on managing changes in your job. Finding career contentment is sometimes mostly dependent on a supportive work environment that values the development of its employees.

Finding a rewarding career may also be accomplished through self-employment and entrepreneurship. Some people find that the independence to launch their own company or pursue a freelancing career better fits their interests, values, and skill set than a regular job. Entrepreneurship gives one more control over their career path and the chance to create a job that is especially suited to their hobbies and areas of strength. That also calls for a great deal of risk management, resilience, and self-motivation, though. Before starting an entrepreneurial endeavor, you must carefully evaluate your abilities, business sense, and market prospects.

Beyond conventional jobs and entrepreneurship, thinking about other employment arrangements can also result in professional contentment. Increased independence and work-life balance may be had via part-time jobs, flexible hours, and remote employment. Examining these possibilities calls for a careful evaluation of your abilities and their applicability in unconventional work settings. New opportunities to build a career that fits with your goals both personally and professionally are presented by the growth of the gig economy and digital nomadism.

Further opportunities to explore and hone talents while supporting worthwhile causes are volunteering and pro bono employment. Volunteering may broaden your professional network, provide you with invaluable experience, and reveal information about possible career routes. A love of community development or social work, for example, may be revealed by volunteering for a nonprofit. Your talents are improved by these encounters, which also give you a feeling of fulfillment and purpose.

In the linked world of today, cultural and worldwide consciousness are becoming more and more crucial. Learning globally applicable talents, including language ability, cross-cultural communication, and international business savvy, may lead to a variety of career options. Studying overseas, working in multicultural settings, or taking part in foreign initiatives are just a few of the international experiences that may expand your viewpoint and improve your skill set. Finding a satisfying career that is enjoyable both personally and professionally may be much aided by this global perspective.

In addition, current professional endeavors need an embrace of technology and digital literacy. Many sectors have been completely changed by the quick progress of technology, which has also brought up new chances and required new abilities. Building your skills in coding, data analysis, digital technologies, and online communication may increase your employability and lead to creative professional opportunities. Finding and pursuing a satisfying career requires you to keep up with technology developments and improve your digital abilities on a regular basis.

Lastly, the capacity for making a good influence is intimately related to work pleasure and fulfillment. Your career might have a greater feeling of purpose if you can see how your abilities can improve society or your neighborhood. Using your talents for the benefit of others may improve your professional fulfillment, whether it be through community service, advocacy work, or corporate social responsibility projects. A great sense of success and happiness may result from matching your work with issues that are important to you and from discovering methods to make a significant contribution.

Finally, evaluating abilities to discover a rewarding career is a complex procedure requiring self-awareness, organized assessments, real-world experiences, ongoing education, and flexibility. It calls for a thorough awareness of your talents, interests, and moral principles, as well as your capacity to match them with career chances. Through reflective practices, feedback seeking, a variety of experiences, and an embrace of lifelong learning, you may choose and follow a career that fulfills you. The path to professional fulfillment is dynamic and continuous and requires tenacity, adaptability, and a dedication to both professional and personal development, whether one chooses traditional employment, entrepreneurship, other work arrangements, or volunteer work. You may design a career path that is satisfying, enriching, and in line with your larger life objectives by matching your talents with worthwhile and enjoyable jobs.

Integrating Ikigai into one's professional life

In Japan, where it is regarded as a means of achieving happiness and a sense of purpose, ikigai is a complex idea with strong cultural origins. Ikigai stresses inner fulfillment and balance, unlike Western ideas of job success, which frequently concentrate on outward accomplishments like money and position. The goal is to combine in a harmonic way the things that satisfy one's material, spiritual, and emotional requirements. As seen by the high life expectancy and perceived well-being of Okinawans, an area where Ikigai is a major component of the culture, this alignment is thought to result in a longer, healthier, and happier life.

The four primary elements of Ikigai—passion, mission, vocation, and profession—must be well understood in order to completely incorporate it into professional life. What you love to do, the things that thrill and motivate you, is called passion. The world needs mission; it includes all the ways you may improve society and change things. What you can be paid for is your career; match your abilities to market demand to guarantee financial security. Your profession is your area of expertise, your acquired skills and abilities.

A happy and well-balanced existence is produced by the meeting point of several elements. Passion and purpose come together to provide excitement and a sense of contribution; yet, if you don't take vocation and career into account, you might find yourself without financial security. When purpose and vocation come together, you support society and make a livelihood, but without enthusiasm and expertise, you may feel empty. Comparably, if your passion and career collide, you may continue to love and be successful at what you do as long as it doesn't satisfy a need in society or bring in money. Finding the perfect balance between all four components is the aim in order to provide a complete feeling of fulfillment and purpose.

Including Ikigai into one's work life starts with introspection and evaluation of oneself. This is figuring out your interests, values, strengths, and passions. Assessments of your personality, talents, and professional preferences include the Myers-Briggs Type Indicator (MBTI), StrengthsFinder, and Holland Code (RIASEC). Analyzing your prior experiences—both personal and professional—can reveal trends in your areas of strength and enjoyment.

Finding your hobbies and strong points can help you determine how they could fit with what the world wants and what you might be compensated for. Researching sectors, jobs, and market trends is a common way to find chances where your hobbies and talents may be put to use meeting society demands. Informational interviews, job shadowing, and networking may provide you insightful knowledge about many career options and show you how others have combined their hobbies with their employment.

A sense of purpose is mostly found when your passion and mission meet. This can include taking up community service, volunteering, or working on initiatives that deal with social concerns that interest you personally. Along with offering fulfillment, these experiences can create chances to network with people and groups that share your ideals and objectives.

Knowing the state of the economy and the market is necessary to align your purpose and vocation and to determine where your talents might be needed. This might be getting more degrees, honing new skills, or changing careers to better fit your interests and the demands of society. Developing professionally and learning new things all help one stay current and flexible in a changing workforce.

Including Ikigai into your work life also entails practical issues like budgeting and work-life balance. Long-term happiness and well-being need that your chosen professional route offer financial security. This might need relocating your job strategically, haggling over pay, and handling your money well to enable the lifestyle you want.

A further important component of incorporating Ikigai is work-life balance. Relationships and personal health should never suffer in order to have a rewarding career. Long-term satisfaction and fulfillment need establishing limits, giving self-care first priority, and striking a good balance between work and personal life. Ikigai integration into professional life may be greatly improved by employers who offer flexible work schedules, health initiatives, and a positive work environment.

Fostering an atmosphere where staff members may follow their Ikigai also heavily depends on the leadership and company culture. Employee happiness and performance may be much impacted by leaders who identify and develop individual talents, promote professional development, and instill a sense of purpose inside the company. Employee values may be matched with and a feeling of purpose can be created by organizational practices that encourage creativity, cooperation, and social responsibility.

As you work toward incorporating Ikigai into your working life, coaching and mentoring are invaluable tools. Mentors may help with professional choices and obstacles by offering direction, sharing experiences, and encouragement. People can benefit from career coaches in helping them to express their objectives, create doable strategies, and maintain attention on their long-term objectives. A vital part may be played by both coaches and mentors in assisting people in coordinating their values, talents, and career path.

One's work life and Ikigai are dynamically and continuously integrated processes. It calls for ongoing introspection, flexibility, and a readiness to welcome change. People change as people do; their interests, talents, and situations may also, hence their Ikigai must be periodically reevaluated and realigned. It takes accepting this flexibility and being receptive to fresh chances and experiences to have a happy and purposeful career.

Ikigai integration into work life can also have effects that go beyond personal satisfaction. Companies who help staff members identify and follow their Ikigai stand to gain from higher levels of retention, productivity, and engagement. Motivated, creative, and dedicated to the company's vision are employees that experience a sense of purpose and alignment with their job. This establishes a positive feedback loop in which success of the person and the organization reinforces one another.

The ideas of Ikigai can help to solve societal issues in the global setting by matching personal skills and interests with more general society demands. More people choosing careers that tackle important problems like social justice, public health, and environmental sustainability, the more people working together to effect good change. This emphasizes the possibilities of Ikigai as a framework for both individual fulfillment and society advancement.

Corporate social responsibility (CSR) and also the incorporation of Ikigai into work life also overlap. Social and environmental responsible companies can provide their staff members chances to work on worthwhile projects that are in line with their beliefs. By giving staff members avenues to support organizations they support, CSR programs may help them feel more purposeful and connected to their jobs. Individual and corporate ideals aligning like this can improve work satisfaction and loyalty generally.

Application of Ikigai concepts can also promote mental health and wellbeing at work. Positive psychological results including less stress, more resilience, and general well-being have been associated with a feeling of purpose and alignment with one's job. Organizations may help create healthier, more encouraging work cultures by creating settings where staff members can follow their Ikigai.

Including Ikigai into work life also means accepting variety and inclusivity. Finding one's own Ikigai may be made possible and the workplace can be enhanced by acknowledging and appreciating other skills, viewpoints, and experiences. Supporting various work styles, career routes, and personal situations, inclusive policies may help all employees succeed and feel fulfilled.

All things considered, incorporating Ikigai into one's work life calls for a comprehensive strategy that harmonizes one's own interests, abilities, morals, and society demands. Through introspection, ongoing education, and strategic planning, one may find and follow professional routes that offer both financial security and fulfillment. Sustaining long-term happiness requires practical factors including work-life balance, financial preparation, and flexibility. Supporting staff members in pursuing their Ikigai depends critically on the culture of the organization, the leadership, the mentoring, and the inclusive policies. Ikigai's wider ramifications include success of organizations, advancement of society, mental health, and well-being, underscoring its potential as a revolutionary paradigm for both personal and group satisfaction. Adopting the Ikigai concepts can result in a work life that is purposeful, balanced, and meaningful, which will eventually make the workforce more resilient, creative, and involved.

CHAPTER V

Living Ikigai in Daily Life

Incorporating Ikigai into daily life practices

Ikigai's core is understood by in-depth introspection. It demands people examine their own interests, talents, morals, and goals. Many tools and methods for self-evaluation might help in this reflective process. Personality tests such as the Big Five Personality Traits or the Myers-Briggs Type Indicator (MBTI) assist people in comprehending their innate inclinations and how they may affect job decisions. Tests of strengths, including the CliftonStrengths (formerly StrengthsFinder), pinpoint a person's greatest strengths and how to use them to succeed and be happy at work.

Finding your passions—things and hobbies that really thrill and inspire you—is an essential component of introspection. Understanding your actual interests might come from thinking back on the times you felt most alive and involved. This may be considering former jobs when you were really happy and satisfied, charity work, or hobbies. Ikigai is incomplete without passion since it inspires drive and tenacity.

Realizing your strengths—those talents and qualities in which you are naturally gifted—is just as crucial. Both technical proficiency and leadership and communication are examples of soft talents. In order to evaluate your strengths, you must not only reflect but also ask mentors, peers, and supervisors for their unbiased opinions of your skills. Finding jobs where you can perform very well and develop a sense of expertise and mastery is made easier when you know your capabilities.

A further important thing to think about is values. They stand for the things that, in life and work, matter most to you—autonomy, inventiveness, financial stability, or having a good social influence. Making your principles clear guarantees that your professional decisions support your long-term objectives and basic convictions. Finding and ranking your work values may be accomplished with the use of tools such as the O*NET Work Importance Locator or the Work Values Matcher.

Examining how your passions, talents, and values could fit with what the world needs is the next step after you have a good grasp of them. Researching several sectors, social concerns, and new trends is part of this process to find chances where your special talents and interests might be applied to solve practical problems. Practical experience and a better grasp of society's needs can be gained by volunteering, interning, or working on community initiatives. Together with helping you pinpoint areas where you may have a significant influence, these activities also help you network and create possible job prospects.

A strong tactic in the search for a job that fits with Ikigai is networking. Developing contacts with experts in your area of interest may offer insightful advice, chances for teamwork, and insightful mentoring. Joining professional groups, going to industry conferences, and using online platforms like LinkedIn might help you meet others who are passionate about the same things you are. Additionally, useful methods to learn about several career options and get firsthand knowledge of different positions are informational interviews and work shadowing.

Getting your Ikigai is mostly dependent on mentoring. Mentors may offer direction, encouragement, and counsel based on their own experiences. They are frequently seasoned experts in the area you want to work. They can support you in negotiating obstacles, establishing reasonable objectives, and creating plans for professional growth. Along with support and inspiration, a good mentor can keep you concentrated and dedicated to your long-term goals.

Apart from locating a job that is in line with Ikigai, it is also possible and frequently required to design a career that satisfies these values. The employment market of today is dynamic and perpetually changing. Hence classic career routes might not always exactly fit your Ikigai. Opportunities to build positions and companies that fit your interests, talents, and values are presented via entrepreneurship and intrapreneurship.

Entrepreneurship is launching your own company or endeavor. This route enables you to produce value in ways that satisfy society's demands, select projects that match your passions, and mold your work environment. Because they can completely incorporate what they love, what they are excellent at, and what the world needs into their everyday job, successful entrepreneurs frequently discover that their businesses are a direct extension of their Ikigai. But being an entrepreneur also calls for fortitude, flexibility, and a readiness to take calculated chances. Creating a network of peers, mentors, and advisers who support one another can assist one in negotiating the difficulties of entrepreneurship.

Conversely, intrapreneurship promotes an entrepreneurial attitude inside a current company. This might be heading creative initiatives, pushing for reform, or creating new goods and services that complement your Ikigai. Through intrapreneurship, you may follow your passions and meet society's needs while using the resources and backing of a well-established company. It calls for both initiative and the capacity to motivate and inspire people in the company.

Maintaining alignment with your Ikigai across your career requires professional growth and ongoing education. The work market of today requires a continual flux of information and abilities, hence it is essential to keep up with developments and trends in the sector. Continuing your education, earning credentials, going to seminars, and taking online classes may all assist you acquire new skills and adjust to new chances. Beyond improving your professional skills, lifelong learning keeps you interested and driven in your work.

Including Ikigai in your working life also requires careful consideration of work-life balance. Relationships and one's own health should not suffer for rewarding work. Burnout may be avoided and general contentment maintained by giving self-care, limits, and time for family and personal hobbies top priority. Workers' capacity to pursue their Ikigai can be greatly increased by employers who provide flexible work schedules, wellness initiatives, and a positive work environment.

A job that fits with Ikigai also heavily depends on financial planning. Long-term happiness requires that your chosen work path satisfy your lifestyle demands and offer financial security. This might need negotiating pay, moving strategically in your work, and handling money well. Making educated choices regarding job options and financial planning can be facilitated by knowing the state of the economy and the market need for your talents.

Including diversity and inclusiveness in your work life is another aspect of integrating Ikigai. Finding one's own Ikigai may be made possible, and the workplace can be enhanced by acknowledging and appreciating other skills, viewpoints, and experiences. Supporting various work styles, career routes, and personal situations, inclusive policies may help all employees succeed and feel fulfilled.

An atmosphere where staff members may follow their Ikigai is mostly dependent on the leadership and company culture. Employee happiness and performance may be much impacted by leaders who identify and develop individual talents, promote professional development, and instill a sense of purpose inside the company. Collaborative, innovative, and socially conscious organizational practices can be in line with the values of the workforce and strengthen the feeling of purpose among all of them.

Furthermore, there are more consequences of incorporating Ikigai into work life than just personal satisfaction. Companies that help staff members identify and follow their Ikigai stand to gain from higher levels of retention, productivity, and engagement. Motivated, creative, and dedicated to the company's vision are employees who experience a sense of purpose and alignment with their jobs. This establishes a positive feedback loop in which the success of the person and the organization reinforces one another.

By bringing personal skills and interests into line with more general social demands, the Ikigai principles can also help to address society's problems. The more people choose careers that tackle important problems like social justice, public health, and environmental sustainability, the more people work together to effect good change. This emphasizes Ikigai's promise as a foundation for both individual fulfillment and societal advancement.

Including Ikigai into work life also touches on the idea of corporate social responsibility (CSR). Social and environmental responsible companies can provide their staff members chances to work on worthwhile projects that are in line with their beliefs. By giving staff members avenues to support organizations they support, CSR programs may help them feel more purposeful and connected to their jobs. Individual and corporate ideals aligning like this can improve work satisfaction and loyalty generally.

Applying the Ikigai concepts can also help with mental health and well-being at work. Positive psychological results including less stress, more resilience, and general well-being, have been associated with a feeling of purpose and alignment with one's job. Organizations may help to create a healthier, more encouraging work culture by creating settings where staff members can follow their Ikigai.

Accepting the idea of a "career lattice" as opposed to a "career ladder" is another aspect of integrating Ikigai into professional life. Although traditional career pathways frequently stress upward mobility and linear advancement, in practice careers can go in many different directions. A career lattice method enables lateral moves, changes between industries, and ongoing adjustment to new prospects. This adaptability may improve the chance of landing and keeping a job that fits with Ikigai.

Professional life integration of Ikigai also calls for a proactive and deliberate strategy. It entails establishing specific objectives, creating doable strategies, and often evaluating and realigning your professional route with your changing interests, talents, and moral principles. To maintain long-term contentment, one must embrace change and be receptive to fresh experiences and chances.

Ultimately, identifying or developing a job that fits with Ikigai calls for a comprehensive and dynamic strategy that combines networking, strategic planning, self-reflection, and ongoing education. The basis of this path is realizing your interests, talents, values, and society demands. Finding and going after employment possibilities that fit with your Ikigai requires networking, mentoring, and professional growth. Create jobs and companies that satisfy your Ikigai through intrapreneurship and entrepreneurship. Long-term happiness and well-being need work-life balance, financial preparation, and a positive corporate culture. The Ikigai concepts have wider ramifications for company performance, society advancement, and mental wellness, in addition to helping people feel fulfilled personally. Ikigai can help people and companies live balanced, purposeful, and purpose-driven working lives, which will eventually result in a more creative, resilient, and engaged workforce.

Cultivating mindfulness and gratitude

Two very effective techniques that may greatly improve mental, emotional, and physical well-being are mindfulness and gratitude. A more harmonious, balanced, and satisfying existence is built on these interrelated and mutually reinforcing behaviors. The ideas of mindfulness and thankfulness are examined in this section along with their advantages and doable methods for integrating them into day-to-day living to develop greater awareness and appreciation.

Being totally in the present and judgment-free, conscious of one's thoughts, feelings, physical sensations, and surroundings, is known as mindfulness. Mindfulness has been embraced broadly in secular settings and included in a number of therapeutic and wellness techniques. Mindfulness is essentially attention and awareness, which is watching events as they happen in the present moment without becoming sidetracked by regrets from the past or worries about the future.

The well-researched advantages of mindfulness extend throughout a number of facets of health and well-being. Because mindfulness encourages relaxation and serenity, it can help to lower stress. Through attention to the here and now, people can break the loop of unfavorable thought patterns that frequently lead to tension and worry. Studies have indicated that mindfulness helps lessen symptoms of anxiety and depression, as well as cortisol, the stress hormone.

By making one more aware of their emotions and allowing room between input and reaction, mindfulness also improves emotional control. Because of their increased awareness, people may react to circumstances more carefully than impulsively. By encouraging empathy, compassion, and improved communication, mindfulness may thus enhance relationships.

Physically, by lessening chronic pain symptoms, boosting immune system function, and promoting better sleep, mindfulness can benefit general health. By urging mindful eating and exercise, the approach promotes a healthy lifestyle that can improve cardiovascular health and weight control.

By contrast, gratitude is the act of identifying and valuing the good things in life. It is recognizing our blessings, the people who support our health, and the chances and encounters that make life more meaningful. Gratitude is an attitude and a way of perceiving the world that may be developed by deliberate activities; it is more than just an emotion.

Thanksfulness has many and deep advantages. Through the promotion of good feelings, raising life satisfaction, and lessening of anxiety and depression symptoms, gratitude can improve mental health. People that concentrate on their blessings divert their attention from unfavorable ideas and events, which might result in a more optimistic view of life.

Through its promotion of prosocial actions and enhancement of connections, gratitude also fosters social ties. Thanking others for their support and connection helps improve those sentiments. More willing to perform deeds of kindness, grateful people can start a beneficial feedback cycle of generosity and friendliness.

Gratitude might also help one feel better physically. Those that are grateful tend to look after themselves better by doing things like exercising on a regular basis, having a healthy diet, and getting enough sleep. Longer life, better immune system function, and reduced blood pressure have all been linked to gratitude.

With all of mindfulness and gratitude's advantages, including these techniques in daily living can result in a more resilient, balanced, and satisfying existence. The parts that follow offer a thorough manual for integrating mindfulness and gratitude into daily life by examining doable techniques for developing these habits.

Meditation is one useful method of developing mindfulness. Sitting quietly, one practices mindfulness meditation by concentrating on their breath, their body, or a particular object of attention. The technique is gentle and judgment-free, returning the attention to the present moment when the mind strays, as it will unavoidably do. Frequent mindfulness meditation helps with emotional stability, stress reduction, and attention. A few minutes a day at first, then progressively longer, can help to make the practice more manageable and long-lasting.

Mindful breathing is an alternative method of mindfulness practice. Anyone, at any moment, may perform this easy yet effective exercise. Those who can stay in the present moment can pay great attention to how their breath enters and leaves their body. Stress and anxiety can be especially well-served by mindful breathing, which offers a rapid and efficient means of regaining clarity and calm.

An interesting mindfulness technique called body scan meditation is methodically concentrating on various body parts, from the head to the toes. Through the profound relaxation and body awareness this technique fosters, people may let go of stress and become more in touch with their bodily feelings. Particularly helpful for people who suffer from persistent pain or discomfort is body scan meditation.

Practices of mindful movement, including qigong, tai chi, and yoga, integrate physical exercise with awareness. Focusing on the breath, these exercises call for awareness of the body's motions, sensations, and alignment. Movement done mindfully may increase strength, flexibility, and balance while encouraging presence and serenity. Frequent deliberate exercise can improve health on the inside as much as outside.

Apart from official mindfulness techniques, regular tasks may be greatly improved by including mindfulness. Eating mindfully is observing food's flavor, texture, and scent as well as the eating process itself. Improved digestion, healthier eating habits, and a deeper enjoyment of food can all result from this exercise. Similar awareness of the sensations of walking—such as the feel of the ground beneath the feet and the movement of the legs—is required for mindful walking. A basic stroll may become a grounding and peaceful experience with this technique.

One may also meaningfully include gratitude exercises in everyday life in a number of ways. One well-used and successful technique is to keep a thankfulness notebook.

Spend a little time each day writing down three to five things for which you are thankful. These might be little or large, from common joys to momentous life experiences. Thinking back on these good things might help you to turn your attention from what isn't there in your life to what is plenty.

Thanking others is a potent additional thankfulness exercise. Words spoken aloud, messages in writing, or deeds of generosity can all do this. It can improve relationships and promote a feeling of togetherness to take the time to thank someone for their help, compassion, or efforts. Gratitude improves the recipient's life as well as the one expressing it.

During a gratitude meditation, you concentrate on your blessings and let yourself really feel and enjoy these wonderful emotions. This technique may be included in regular activities or performed during a structured meditation session. A little time spent before bed, for instance, considering the benefits of the day might help one feel peaceful and pleased.

By deliberate appreciation, one can also develop mindfulness and thankfulness. With this exercise, you deliberately seek out and value the good things in your life and surroundings. To increase your sense of thankfulness and presence, for example, pause to enjoy a stunning sunset, the sound of birds chirping, and also the warmth of the sun on your skin.

Practices of mindfulness and thankfulness may work together powerfully to enhance the advantages of each. You may concentrate on thankfulness during a mindfulness meditation practice, for instance, and let these good sensations enhance your awareness of your presence and well-being. Alternatively, to improve your whole experience, you might be conscious of the feelings and emotions that surface when practicing thankfulness.

It needs a supportive setting to encourage mindfulness and thankfulness exercises. This is making time and space set apart, distraction-free, for these exercises. Making gratitude and mindfulness exercises a regular part of your life might be facilitated by creating a schedule. A regular and grounded routine may be established, for example, by spending a few minutes either at the beginning or end of the day in mindfulness meditation or gratitude reflection.

Gratitude and mindfulness activities can also be supported by group or community involvement. Taking part in gratitude challenges, attending mindfulness seminars, or joining a meditation group may all help one feel motivated, accountable, and part of a larger mission. Membership in a group of people who share your values may also provide insightful advice, encouragement, and support.

Gratitude and mindfulness integration in daily living calls for perseverance, dedication, and practice. Approaching these exercises with an open and nonjudgmental mindset is crucial, understanding that there may be ups and downs and that progress may be slow. Gratitude and mindfulness both depend heavily on being kind and compassionate with oneself, particularly when things are tough or frustrating.
Creative pursuits may help one develop mindfulness and appreciation as well. Writing, painting, or other creative expression can help people achieve a condition of flow, in which they are totally absorbed and in the present. Together with giving one a way to express and process emotions, these pursuits can help one to recognize and enjoy the richness and beauty of life.

Gratitude and mindfulness may come from nature in great measure. Whether in a park, forest, beach or garden, spending time in the natural world may heighten emotions of amazement, gratitude and wonder.

Gardening, doing nature hikes, or just spending time in the great outdoors taking in the sights, sounds, and fragrances can all be quite reviving and grounding.

Relationships are another setting in which to develop mindfulness and appreciation. It can improve relationships and mutual understanding and support to be really present with people, listen carefully, and value their presence and contributions. In partnerships, expressing thankfulness may start a loving and appreciative loop that strengthens closeness and trust.

It is possible to live gratefully and mindfully even in our regular activities and jobs. When one approaches work mindfully, one is totally present and concentrated on the task at hand, not sidetracked by multitasking or future worries. Productivity, inventiveness, and pleasure may all be increased by this. Discovering things about work for which we are thankful, including chances for development, teamwork, or the chance to further a greater good, can completely change how we see our careers.

One way to include mindfulness and appreciation into our everyday lives is to declutter and simplify both our mental and physical environments. More room is created for conscious presence and appreciation when we cut down on pointless distractions and concentrate on what is important. This might include arranging our living and work spaces, establishing clear priorities, and giving up on pursuits or obligations that go against our ideals and objectives.

Technology may help with mindfulness and appreciation exercises as well as present obstacles. Though too much screen time and digital distractions can be detrimental to mindful living, there are plenty of applications and internet resources accessible to help with these techniques. Online diaries, mindfulness and meditation tools, and virtual mindfulness groups may offer direction, organization, and encouragement for developing mindfulness and appreciation.

Developing mindfulness and thankfulness is ultimately a lifetime endeavor requiring ongoing education, experience, and modification. Developing a deeper and more compassionate connection with ourselves, others, and the environment around us is the goal of these techniques, not reaching a flawless state of mind. Our foundation for a more robust, healthy, and satisfying existence may be laid by practicing mindfulness and gratitude.

Finally, gratitude and mindfulness are transforming techniques that may greatly improve general well-being. Through the promotion of greater awareness and presence, these techniques can lower stress, strengthen relationships, enhance emotional control, and improve physical health. Using meditation and mindful breathing to gratitude writing and thanking others are just a few of the doable techniques for incorporating mindfulness and gratitude into everyday living. To increase the advantages of these techniques, one may establish a supportive atmosphere, interact with a community, and include them in work, relationships, and artistic pursuits. A life-enriching and profoundly rewarding activity, mindfulness and gratitude cultivation is a lifelong process of development, learning, and adaptability.

Navigating challenges and finding resilience through Ikigai

Recognizing the fundamental elements of Ikigai is the first step in applying it to solve problems. The four components of Ikigai—passion, mission, vocation, and profession—offer a comprehensive method for discovering one's calling. Passionate pursuits are those that make one happy and satisfied. The mission is attending to society's needs and advancing the greater good. It is about using abilities and skills in ways that other people respect that is called vocation. A career guarantees stable finances by providing worthwhile employment. Through analysis of these elements, people may understand their own Ikigai and how it fits with the circumstances of their lives.

Finding your Ikigai calls for a great deal of contemplation and insight. Throughout this procedure, you will be posed basic questions on your interests, talents, morals, and desired global influence. This investigation may benefit much from journaling. Writing down your ideas and encounters helps you to find trends and understanding that expose your actual goals and driving forces. Thinking back on your experiences—both good and bad—can also reveal what important to you is and how you could use your talents and interests to meet needs in the actual world.

Implementing your Ikigai into your everyday life comes next once you have found it. This integration needs deliberate effort and dedication to coordinate your actions with your main goals and values. Time blocking and prioritizing are two time management strategies that could help you plan your day such that they include things that support your Ikigai. If writing is your passion and your goal is to educate people, for example, you can set aside a certain amount of time every day to work on books or articles that teach. By giving these tasks top importance, you may be confident that your everyday efforts support your sense of purpose in general.

The juggling of obligations to one's family, job, and personal life is one of the biggest problems people encounter. Ikigai offers a direction for striking this equilibrium. Making a clear definition of your priorities can help you decide how best to spend your time and effort. Burnout may be avoided, and you can make sure you have the resources to concentrate on what is important by establishing limits and declining activities that do not fit with your Ikigai. Participating in your Ikigai journey with your family and loved ones may also help to establish a supportive atmosphere where every one's wants and goals are taken into account.

Adapting to and flourishing in the face of hardship is resilience. Strong direction and purpose from ikagai may greatly increase resilience. When your Ikigai is really important to you, you will naturally want to overcome obstacles and disappointments. Even amid trying external conditions, this inherent drive may keep you focused and driven. Furthermore, living in accordance with your Ikigai can serve as a buffer against stress and unpleasant feelings, therefore enhancing general mental and emotional health.

Growing a growth mentality is one doable approach to using Ikigai to develop resilience. With this kind of thinking, obstacles and disappointments become chances for development rather than dangers to your value. Accepting a growth mentality allows you to look for opportunities to change and progress while approaching challenges with openness and curiosity. This viewpoint may turn disappointments into worthwhile experiences that advance your career and personal growth. A growth mentality also promotes empowerment and agency as you understand that, with hard work and persistence, you can change the results.

Resilience also heavily depends on self-care. Keeping your energy and ability to pursue your Ikigai depends on taking care of your physical, emotional, and mental health. Regular exercise, a good diet, enough sleep, and mindfulness exercises like deep breathing and meditation may all be part of this self-care. Giving self-care first priority guarantees that you will be strong and resilient enough to overcome obstacles and carry on pursuing your goals. Self-care routines can also improve your general health and make it simpler to maintain your enthusiasm and drive.

An additional important Ikigai technique for overcoming obstacles and developing resilience is to create a supporting group. Assembling a circle of friends and family who share your interests and ideals might help you feel like you belong. This group may provide you with support, criticism, and tools to keep you on course and get beyond setbacks. Moreover, interacting with people who are also following their Ikigai might inspire and open your eyes to fresh viewpoints, therefore enhancing your own path. Building these relationships—through official organizations, virtual communities, or unofficial networks —can improve your fortitude and sense of direction.

Managing obstacles with Ikigai also requires flexibility and adaptation. Life is, by its very nature, erratic, and things may change fast. Even in the midst of uncertainty, you may stay in line with your Ikigai by being receptive to new chances and prepared to change your plans as needed. This adaptability calls on a readiness to let go of inflexible expectations and welcomes the unforeseen. Staying flexible allows you to develop fresh approaches to follow your goals and have a good influence by gracefully and resiliently navigating changes and obstacles.

Resilience may be increased by the potent practice of gratitude, which changes your attention from what is missing to what is plentiful in your life. Continually recognizing and valuing the good things in your life helps you to develop an abundant and satisfied attitude. This exercise may be as simple as spending a few minutes each day thinking back on what you are grateful for or as detailed in a gratitude notebook. It is easier to remain driven and resilient in the midst of difficulties when one has a positive mindset, which gratitude promotes.

Building resilience through Ikigai also benefits from mindfulness. Being totally in the now, observant of your thoughts, emotions, and environment without passing judgment, is mindfulness. Frequent mindfulness exercises help to lower stress, improve emotional control, and advance general well-being. Through the practice of mindfulness, you may become more conscious of your Ikigai and how it shows itself in your everyday life. Even under trying circumstances, this awareness may keep you centered and grounded and assist you in keeping a strong sense of purpose.

Resilience and also flexibility in a world that is changing quickly need ongoing education and personal growth. You guarantee that you are always developing and changing, both personally and professionally, by committing to lifelong learning. Seeking fresh information, abilities, and experiences that complement your Ikigai can be part of this dedication. Whether you study in a classroom setting, online, in seminars, or on your own, being inquisitive and receptive to new possibilities may improve your capacity for problem-solving and resilience. In addition, ongoing education promotes accomplishment and advancement, which enhances your general feeling of meaning and contentment.

Resilience also heavily weighs financial stability. Though money by itself cannot produce pleasure, financial stability gives you the means and the flexibility to follow your Ikigai without undue worry or stress. This stability includes having sensible money management, reasonable financial objectives, and well-informed spending and saving choices. Keeping your financial habits in line with your goals and beliefs will help to guarantee that your resources promote resilience and general well-being.

Because spiritual activities give one a sense of connectedness to something bigger than oneself, they can also help to increase resilience. Spirituality may provide solace, direction, and inspiration whether practiced through religious traditions, meditation, the natural world, or individual practices. Growing a spiritual practice that is in line with your Ikigai will help you feel more purposeful in life and find support and strength when things become tough. Spiritual activities can also help one experience inner calm and clarity, which facilitates resilience and focus.

A further important element in developing resilience through Ikigai is work-life balance. More than mere success in one's profession, a meaningful life includes time for self-care and leisure, as well as personal connections and interests. Making sure you give everything in your life enough of your time and effort keeps you from burning out and promotes general health. Setting limits between professional and personal time, using good time management techniques, and choosing purposefully how to spend your leisure time are all part of striking this balance. You may improve your resilience and feeling of contentment generally by living a balanced life that represents your Ikigai.

Fundamental to Ikigai is adopting a service and contributing mentality. Finding and living your mission depends critically on knowing how your talents and interests may meet the needs of the world. Little deeds of kindness done every day to major programs and efforts are all possible expressions of this service. By concentrating on how you might improve the lives of others, you develop a sense of fulfillment and purpose that transcends personal pleasure. Service and contribution may also have a good knock-on impact that motivates others and strengthens a feeling of camaraderie and connection.

Finally, overcoming obstacles and developing resilience of with Ikigai calls for a comprehensive and dynamic strategy that combines self-analysis, deliberate action, community support, ongoing education, self-care, gratitude, mindfulness, flexibility, financial security, spirituality, work-life balance, and a service and contribution mentality. When your everyday actions are in line with your beliefs, interests, strengths, and the needs of the world, you build a resilient, purposeful existence. The benefits of this path are great—a very fulfilling and meaningful existence that connects with your actual self and has a good effect on the world around you—but it demands constant self-awareness, intention, and flexibility. The pursuit of their own "reason for being" can provide people the courage and purpose they need to gracefully and resiliently negotiate life's obstacles.

Building habits and routines that support Ikigai

The idea of Ikigai has drawn a lot of interest in the quest for a happy and purposeful existence, especially from people who are engaged in personal development. Japanese in origin, Ikigai is frequently translated as "a reason to wake up in the morning" or "a reason for being." It stands for the meeting point of your talents, what the world needs, what you want to do, and what you can get paid. A happy, balanced existence that fits with one's interests, abilities, and values might result from forming habits and routines that promote Ikigai. Building such habits and routines is complex, as this section explores the psychological foundations, cultural relevance, and doable actions to include Ikigai in daily life.

Understanding the four main elements of Ikigai—passion, purpose, vocation, and profession—is necessary. Interests and talents are the sources of passion. What the world needs and what you love come together in mission. What the world needs and what you can be compensated for lead to vocation. What you can be compensated for and what you are skilled at is your profession. These components coming together provide the basis of Ikigai.

But reaching this balance takes time and conscious efforts to develop suitable routines and habits; it is not a one-time event.

The study of behavior modification provides the psychological foundation for habit-building. A trigger, a routine, and a reward make up habits, claims Charles Duhigg, author of "The Power of Habit." Constructing behaviors that promote Ikigai requires an understanding of this cycle. The activity is initiated by the cue, it is repeated more likely by the reward, and it is the behavior itself. To fit with Ikigai, habits must be carefully designed to speak to the essential elements of passion, purpose, vocation, and profession.

Building behaviors that encourage Ikigai can be accomplished by beginning with little, doable adjustments. This is consistent with the idea of "Kaizen," a Japanese term for ongoing development by little, gradual stages. Those should concentrate on little behaviors that progressively result in big improvements rather than trying to make big changes. If writing is part of your Ikigai, for example, begin with spending just 10 minutes a day on it. With time, this little dedication can increase, making the habit less demanding and more durable.

A further important component of using habits to assist Ikigai is awareness. Being present and giving their activities their whole attention when one is attentive improves their sense of happiness and contentment. Meditation and other mindfulness exercises can be included in regular schedules to keep people concentrated on their Ikigai. Regularly considering their deeds and objectives allows people to make sure that their habits support their larger goals and make necessary adjustments.

Additionally important to maintaining Ikigai is physical health. Keeping up a healthy lifestyle via frequent exercise, well-balanced diet, and enough sleep guarantees that people have the energy and vigor to follow their passions and accomplish their goals. Walking, yoga, or any other kind of exercise one loves may be included into daily schedules to support general well-being. A diet heavy in veggies, lean meats, and whole foods can also supply the essential elements to promote mental and physical wellness.

Ikigai also depends critically on social ties. A feeling of purpose and belonging is much enhanced by establishing and preserving connections with family, friends, and community members. One's Ikigai can be improved by habits that support these connections, including as frequent contact, deeds of kindness, and involvement in community events. A great sense of contentment and happiness may be obtained from having long talks, spending time with loved ones, and improving the lives of others.

To reach Ikigai, one must also constantly study and develop personally. People who participate in mentally taxing and knowledge-expansion activities are more likely to remain inspired and committed to their goals. Reading, enrolling in classes, going to seminars, or just trying out new interests might all be part of it. Lifelong learning is a habit that guarantees people stay inquisitive and receptive to new experiences, which is essential for preserving a feeling of purpose and enthusiasm.

One's feeling of Ikigai may also be much improved by including appreciation into everyday activities. Those who routinely recognize and value the good things in life might develop a more upbeat and contented attitude. This may be accomplished by rituals like journaling your thankfulness, thanking people, and considering your life's blessings. Reiterating a positive attitude and a greater sense of fulfillment, gratitude helps to turn attention from what is missing to what is plentiful.

A further crucial factor to take into account while developing behaviors that promote Ikigai is financial security. Ikigai understands the need to make a livelihood, even as it stresses the value of passion and purpose. Developing financial health-promoting behaviors, like saving, budgeting, and careful spending, may ease stress and provide one the stability they need to follow their real passions. Long-term ambitions should be supported by financial habits, which should also make sure that the pursuit of worthwhile hobbies is not eclipsed by financial worries.

To keep an Ikigai viable, work and play must be balanced. Burnout may arise from working too much and lack of direction from too much leisure. Setting up a schedule that permits both restorative rest and leisure time as well as productive work is finding balance. Creating limits for work hours, planning frequent breaks, and making time for leisure and hobbies could all be part of this. All facets of life are attended to when there is a balanced schedule, which enhances general happiness and well-being.

Ikigai is supported in part by environmental elements as well. One may follow their passions more easily if one creates a physical environment that encourages creativity and production. This may include arranging a workstation, cutting down on outside noise, and surrounding oneself with positive and inspirational things. The efficacy of habits and routines one develops can be greatly impacted by an atmosphere that fosters concentration and creativity.

Moreover, to make sure habits and routines support one's Ikigai, they should be reviewed and modified on a regular basis. It takes flexibility to adjust to changes in priorities and life situations. People may maintain alignment with their Ikigai and make required changes to their routines and habits by routinely reflecting and reevaluating. This might include defining new objectives, assessing current ones, or looking into uncharted territory and chances.

There is no universal method to include Ikigai into daily living. The path of every person is different, and so are the customs and practices that help Ikigai. Throughout this procedure, one should be kind and patient with oneself. It takes constant work, thought, and modification to develop behaviors that promote Ikigai; it is a lifetime endeavor.

Finally, creating routines and habits that promote Ikigai calls for a complex strategy that combines profession, purpose, mission, and passion. Through knowledge of the psychological processes underlying habit formation, small adjustments are made gradually, mindfulness practice, physical health maintained, social connections fostered, lifelong learning, gratitude practice, financial stability ensured, work and leisure balance maintained, environment optimized, and routines routinely reevaluated, people can design a lifestyle that is in line with their Ikigai. This all-encompassing method promotes happiness and personal fulfillment as well as a feeling of direction and significance in life. Living a life in line with one's actual purpose has incalculable benefits, but the path to Ikigai is a continuous process that calls for commitment and self-awareness.

CONCLUSION

"Ikigai Unveiled: The Japanese Secret to a Purposeful Life" offers a deep investigation of the age-old Japanese philosophy of Ikigai and shows how it may change contemporary living. The book carefully analyzes passion, purpose, vocation, and profession—the four fundamental components of Ikigai—and shows how a life well-balanced and incredibly gratifying can result from their harmonic integration. The writers lead readers on a path of self-discovery and personal development by fusing psychological concepts, cultural insights, and useful counsel.

Emphasizing Ikigai's accessibility and simplicity is one of the book's major achievements. It busts the misconception that locating one's Ikigai is an impossible undertaking best left to the wise few. Rather, it demonstrates how everyone can achieve Ikigai as long as they are prepared to reflect, practice mindfulness, and make little changes to their everyday lives. In keeping with the Japanese idea of Kaizen, or ongoing development, the story exhorts readers to begin small, which makes the quest of Ikigai more doable and less intimidating.

Additionally stressed throughout the book is the value of integration and balance. It emphasizes that real fulfillment results from achieving a balance between many aspects of life rather than from focusing on one area of life to the detriment of others. By using a comprehensive strategy, people may be sure that while following their interests and purpose, they do not compromise their relationships, personal development, physical health, or financial security. Through offering doable techniques for juggling work and play, fostering social relationships, and preserving physical and mental health, "Ikigai Unveiled" provides a thorough manual for leading a fulfilling life.

The book's examination of mindfulness and thankfulness techniques also deepens our grasp of Ikigai. These techniques encourage a good attitude that is essential for long-term pleasure and fulfillment by helping readers remain present and value the experience. Through the incorporation of these activities into regular activities, people can improve their awareness and enjoyment of life, therefore enhancing their feeling of happiness and purpose.

"Ikigai Unveiled" is an instruction handbook on leading a meaningful life as well as a theoretical investigation. Its practical advice and experiences from everyday life provide the idea of Ikigai concrete and understandable form. The book provides readers with a transforming path toward finding and developing their Ikigai, which will eventually result in a more fulfilling and meaningful existence. For everyone looking to find their own calling and have a happy, meaningful life, the book is essentially a lighthouse.

Thank you for buying and reading/ listening to our book. If you found this book useful/ helpful please take a few minutes and leave a review on the platform where you purchased our book. Your feedback matters greatly to us.